Far Eastern
OVEREXPOSURE

 Paul Tweiten

Order this book online at www.trafford.com
or email orders@trafford.com

Most Trafford titles are also available at major online book retailers.

For the purpose of this novel, and in respect for their privacy, the names of most individuals and all companies contained herein have been changed.

Joshua Kodis, Great Falls, Montana for cover and editing of interior photos

Printed in the United States of America.

ISBN: 978-1-4269-9507-1 (sc)
ISBN: 978-1-4269-9506-4 (hc)
ISBN: 978-1-4269-9508-8 (e)

Library of Congress Control Number: 2011960466

Trafford rev. 10/08/2014

 www.trafford.com

North America & international
toll-free: 1 888 232 4444 (USA & Canada)
fax: 812 355 4082

Dedicated in memory of Joe Dill, a once in a lifetime friend that unfortunately passed away far too soon. He is missed, but not forgotten.

Chapter One

The Journey

W hen asked how I got involved with Russia, my usual answer is an unwanted divorce, a soon-to-be ex-wife who said she wished I was on the other side of the world, and three very understanding children. One day, while screaming out her displeasure at having me around, I asked if Russia was far enough away for her. She replied, "Yes, it would be," and the rest is, as we say, history.

My first exposure to Russia was at a Forest Products "Pacific Rim Marketing" Seminar in Seattle, Washington, during December of 1994. Part of this particular program was about the start-up of a Russian-American joint venture involved in a remote logging operation located in the Russian Far East. While sitting at lunch with one of the representatives of the U.S. Company, I got into a discussion about how, other than the language issue, their operation was very similar to what I had been involved in for a number of years in Alaska. We exchanged business cards, and I did not give this much more thought until shortly after my wife informed me of her desire to terminate our current relationship and pursue happiness with someone else. That someone else just happened to be one of my employees, which made life in a small rural town rather awkward. So, in late July of 1995, I was on my way driving across country from Ironwood, Michigan, to the Seattle, Washington, area of my youth. It was here that I would be leaving all my remaining worldly belongings, including a Pontiac Trans Am, inside an eight-foot by fourteen-foot storage shed in Poulsbo.

On the morning of August 3, I boarded the Alaska Airlines flight to Khabarovsk, Russia, from Seattle. In total, the trip took approximately thirteen hours, including deplaning for Customs and Immigrations clearance in Anchorage, Alaska, and a short stopover in Magadan, Russia. An MD-80 is not the most comfortable airplane for long-distance flights, but the flight attendants were very pleasant and did the best they could to ease our pain. At that time, beer and wine were still served without charge, and many of the passengers, some of whom were much more seasoned in travel to Russia than I, took liberal advantage of this benefit. One of these blurry-eyed passengers informed me that arriving drunk was the only way some people could make themselves get off the plane for their upcoming tour of duty. This was especially true with crew members of the fishing fleet and processors working off the coast in this region of the north Pacific. I can't say that I was scared of what was to come, but I was certainly apprehensive since I basically knew nothing about Russia and hadn't really cared to until this time.

After leaving Anchorage, the flight took us over the Susitna River valley, across the spectacular mountains of the Alaska Range, and on to the Kuskokwim River and Yukon River drainages. We flew past Nome, and 1¾ hours later entered Russian air space. Once we were again over land, I was amazed at how similar the Russian countryside looked to areas in Alaska. The high snowcapped mountains and volcanoes of the Kamchatka Peninsula were absolutely beautiful. The rugged coastline of the Khabarovsk Krai reminded me of southeast Alaska. On the approach to Magadan I could see numerous large agricultural areas cleared on the outskirts of town, but no houses. I was told by one of the flight attendants that the primary industries in this region were fishing and mining.

It was raining as the airplane taxied onto the tarmac. The view from the window lacked any significant color. A wide, gray concrete surface led to a dirty white concrete terminal building set against a gray overcast sky. Now, I had experienced turbulence in previous flights but never once the plane had landed. The runway was constructed using large cement slabs linked together to form a surface that made you wonder how in the hell an airplane could survive such abuse. From what I understood, the concept behind this design was in part from wartime strategy. Apparently in case of an air strike, the damaged sections could be easily replaced regardless of weather conditions, and the landing strip made functional again in a minimal amount of time. The take-off from this runway wasn't any smoother than the landing had been, and left teeth rattling and tires vibrating long after leaving the ground.

Flying inland, the vast muskeg-swamp areas and large rivers looked as if I was flying over the Alaskan interior near Fairbanks. Although now sunny, a reddish-gray haze filled the air as we descended into the Khabarovsk area, the result of smoke rising from the numerous small forest fires in the surrounding hills. The immediate area surrounding the city consisted of large swamps, rectangular-shaped farmland, and what looked to be small villages. Later I was to learn that these "villages" were *dachas*, or garden plots used by the residents primarily during the summer months. Khabarovsk itself appeared to have three sections, all of which were dominated by dull gray apartment complexes. Black smoke spewed out from three tall stacks at a large facility located on the northeastern edge of the city.

The landing at the Khabarovsk Airport was no softer than that of Magadan. Upon departing the airplane, we were placed onto an old "bus," which basically was a yellow trailer pulled by an exhaust-spewing KMAZ truck, and taken to the terminal. The process of passing through Customs and Immigrations began in a small crowded room. Although I knew absolutely no Russian and the Immigrations officer did not seem to know English, she was extremely pleasant and very good-looking. I handed her my documents, stood still, and smiled. Once my passport and visa were stamped for entry, I proceeded to the baggage claim area then shuffled everything to the X-ray machine and Customs station. During this time period, travelers were still required to fill out a Customs Declaration Form upon entry. It was necessary to identify not only the amount of money you were carrying but also anything else you had of value such as cameras, watch, jewelry, etc. This form was to be retained while in Russia and then turned in upon departure, along with another Declaration to show that you were taking out less money than you brought in. This also served to verify that your valuables were not acquired in Russia so as not to be subject to a customs duty. The Customs Agent, also a very attractive young woman, circled the items I identified, stamped my Declaration, then looked up as she smiled and motioned me out.

When I passed through the door and into the airport lobby, I didn't know who was going to meet me, but I expected it would at least be someone who spoke English. I was wrong. Standing outside of the Immigration/Baggage Claim area were three Russians wearing well-used business suits and asking every American if he were "Pol." I learned that the individual leading my greeting party was named Sergei. With him was a fourteen-year-old interpreter whose name I couldn't understand, and who, although being a nice kid, knew very little English.

Prior to leaving the terminal, I exchanged $550 US at the airport's currency exchange center, and upon receiving 2,453,000 rubles, chuckled to myself that at last I could claim to be a millionaire. We then loaded my two containers and suitcase into one of two Toyota Coronas parked outside. I hopped into the other car and immediately noticed that the steering wheel was on the wrong side. The driver drove like a maniac, and following a nerve-racking thirty-minute drive, we arrived safely at the train station. Apparently I would not be staying in Khabarovsk, but taking an evening train to where I did not know. Inside the main hall was dirty, crowded, and appeared extremely disorganized. I gave Sergei my documents, and he joined the mob at one of the ticket booths while I stood back and watched the chaos. People were rushing around everywhere, coming and going, pushing and shoving—that is, those who were not just standing around drinking. When he returned with the ticket, I learned my destination was Komsomolsk and that the train departed at 10:00 p.m. To my surprise, I was also told I'd be traveling alone.

With my evening itinerary secured, we hopped back into the car for a short drive to the Intourist Hotel. As we sped along the boulevard, I couldn't help but notice that short skirts and high heels definitely seemed to be in style here. Once checked in, we squeezed into a 3½-foot by 4½-foot elevator, and I was accompanied up to my room. My baggage was left next to the bed, and Sergei then attempted to explain what was going to happen next. However, since he couldn't speak English, I didn't understand Russian, and the kid couldn't really translate, the only thing I could figure out was that I'd be picked up sometime around 9:00 p.m. to go to the train station.

The Russians departed, and I was left alone to freshen up and relax for a couple of hours. The relatively tiny room contained two single beds smaller in size than a twin, two nightstands, a television which showed only three channels, and a mini-refrigerator with nothing in it. The single window provided a nice view overlooking the Amur River toward China. I turned the TV on and was surprised to find an Arnold Schwarzenegger movie. However, "I'll be back" just doesn't come across with the same meaning when being translated in an unenthusiastic Russian monotone. The bathroom was small, about three feet by four feet, with a sink, toilet, and shower. I found it kind of amusing that you could sit on the toilet and take a shower at the same time. The water was lukewarm at best, but after the long trip, it felt good anyway.

Sergei returned to take me to the train station and, considering the panicked rush in getting me checked out and into the car, I assumed we were short on time. At the station, I was led down some stairs into a narrow, damp, dimly lit corridor lined with small kiosks, newspaper stands, and drunks. At the first set of stairs we came to, we climbed back up and outside onto the loading area. After showing the attendant my passport, visa, and ticket, I climbed on board for what was to be my first train ride ever.

The cabin on the train was relatively comfortable, containing a small table and two bench seats, which after the placement of small, heavily stained mattresses, also served as beds. Above each bench was a fold-up "bunk" bed enabling each compartment to sleep a total of four people. I had tickets for two bunks so that my two containers and suitcase could also be accommodated. Shortly after Sergei left and I had settled in, an attractive young girl in her early twenties sat down on the seat across from me. She smiled at me and said something which I figured was Russian for "hello." When I answered "hello" in English, her posture immediately relaxed and her smile grew. She apparently was also traveling to Komsomolsk, and it seemed we were going to be sharing the compartment for the duration of the trip. That was until a young man, whom I assumed was her boyfriend, poked his head in the doorway, took one look at me, then started a heated argument with the girl. He continued to shout his apparent displeasure with the situation, as he walked down the corridor toward the attendant. A few minutes later they both returned, and much to my disappointment, the girl was escorted to another compartment elsewhere on the railcar.

At 10:05 p.m., the train departed to the sound of music blaring from a raspy depot speaker system, which I believe was the same music used to send off soldiers during the Patriotic War (WWII). Just outside of the city, the train rolled through a long tunnel, and after about seven minutes of total darkness, we came out to a beautiful sunset. About twenty minutes later, the train made a stop at a small town, and my new roommates, two older women with two small kids in diapers, came on board. As the train began to move again, I rolled over in my top bunk thinking, "*This could be interesting.*"

Even with the sliding door open, the small compartment was hot and muggy with little if any airflow. As a result, I worked up a sweat just lying there but quickly fell asleep anyway. When I awoke later that night, my roommates were gone.

About an hour prior to our scheduled 7:00 a.m. arrival in Komsomolsk-na-Amur, the attendant knocked, unlocked the door, then shouted something I didn't understand and walked away. I opened the compartment door and saw people in various stages of dress walking up and down the corridor. Others were leaning against the handrail, staring out the windows. I slipped on my jeans then walked to the end of the railcar to wait my turn for the toilet. The facility was small, at best three-feet square, and contained a stainless steel sink with a mirror on the wall above it, a small wastebasket, and stainless steel toilet. Fortunately, I did not require the use of any toilet paper since none was available, only a few "used" pieces of newspaper lay crumpled in the waste basket. I lifted the seat cover, grabbed on to a handle on the wall to control my swaying, and tried to keep my aim within the bowl. Once finished, I stepped on the lever to flush, and it was then I realized that everything dropped directly onto the tracks below.

The weather was sunny and pleasantly warm when I arrived at Komsomolsk. I struggled to get my suitcase and containers down the narrow corridor to the doorway of the railcar. I was again met by three Russians, and of course none of them could speak English. With their assistance, however, I got everything off the train and transferred to two cars parked in front of the station. As we drove through the city, I still had no clue as to what was going on or where I was being taken. Even though it was early in the morning on a Saturday, I was surprised by the lack of activity on the streets. It did strike my interest though as to how wide the streets were. I learned later that this was in part to accommodate the width of MIG jet fighters passing through the streets during parade ceremonies.

After about ten minutes or so, the driver pulled over to the curb and stopped to let another guy into the car. He introduced himself as Jeff Major, an employee of Frontier Investments living there in Komsomolsk. At last, I thought with some relief, somebody who actually spoke English and could tell me what the hell was going on. Jeff informed me that the gentleman sitting in the front seat of the car was Dmitry Sharkoff, the President of the Russian joint venture.

I was taken to a company-owned apartment that was to be my accommodations for the next two days. Once at the apartment complex, we entered the building through a heavy steel door and then through another into the apartment. After placing my baggage in the bedroom, I was given the keys and informed that they would return in a couple of hours to take me to the office. After taking a quick shower, I was beginning to get hungry, so I looked in the refrigerator to see what might be there. Unfortunately, there was not much that I could use other than a couple of bottles of mineral water. I found a box of chocolate candies on a cabinet in the living room, grabbed a couple of granola bars from my container, and sat down to wait for my hosts to return. I didn't understand what was being said, but I turned the television on anyway just to have some noise.

During our short meeting at the office, it became evident that no one had received any prior information on me and why I was there in Russia. Consequently there was, at least among the Russians, some apprehension and anxiety toward me. Following their interrogation and apparently relieving their concerns, they offered to have breakfast cooked up for me. Having only eaten granola bars, Snickers, and chocolates since getting off the airplane, how could I decline? On our way back to the apartment, we stopped at a small grocery store to buy some bread, cheese, juice, and beer.

Not wanting to stay in the apartment after Jeff left, I decided to go out and get some fresh air. As it turned out, the apartment building was not far from a public beach area along the Amur River. It was turning out to be a hot day and quite a few people were already at the beach; some were swimming, but most were just sunbathing. My attention quickly turned to the female sunbathers in their European-style thong bikinis. I don't think that I had ever seen that many beautiful, slim, long-legged bodies in one location ever before. As I sat on the bulkhead drinking a beer and watching the world go by, I thought to myself that maybe Russia wasn't going to be so bad after all! Occasionally a long, skinny hydroplane-type boat would noisily pass by on the river, but other than that, it was quite peaceful. Later in the day, Jeff came by the apartment and invited me back to his apartment to meet his family and have dinner. We were talking about my initial impression of Komsomolsk when Jeff told me that one of the city's main sewer lines dumped untreated raw sewage into the river just upstream from the beach I had visited. I could hardly believe this, since I had even seen people fishing there!

Early Monday morning, I awoke to dogs barking somewhere out in the courtyard and people screaming. This continued for quite some time until suddenly what sounded like a single gunshot rang out, and then everything was quiet. At 8:30 a.m. I was surprised to be taken to the office in a brand-new 1995 Ford extended-cab, 4x4 pickup truck. While being shown around, I was introduced to a number of the Russians I'd be working with. However, most of my morning was spent listening to Jeff complain about the Philadelphia office personnel and policies. Much of the conversation with the Russians was centered on their complaints about the American general manager at Siziman Bay.

I was taken upstairs to a small cafeteria area for lunch, which consisted of some kind of beet salad, vegetable soup, cube steak, a hot dog-type sausage within a bread roll, and juice. In the afternoon, I learned that there was a problem with my visa in that it did not include authorization or identify the appropriate destination point to enable me to legally travel to Siziman Bay. I was assured that they could take care of this issue and taken to a photography shop nearby to obtain photos for a new visa. The photographer's camera was something like I've never seen before, other than in old silent movies. It was probably a 1930s vintage or earlier, the type with the photo plate in the back and a lens cap that is removed for a short period of time to expose the film. Afterward, Jeff commented that the Russians must like me, because they were applying for a one-year multiple-entry visa rather than the usual three-month single-entry visa normally given to expats.

When it was finally time to head to the train station the next day, my belongings as well as an additional container full of equipment parts were loaded into the back of the Ford. I was later told that Russian customs officials considered this truck to be a "luxury" vehicle due to it having seat belts in the rear passenger area. Subsequently, with the initial purchase price of the vehicle, ocean freight, increased customs duty, rail transportation, etc., the final "in Komsomolsk" cost of the truck was in excess of $100,000. During this trip, I would not be traveling alone but was joined by Andrei Chekinkov, a Russian forester, and his twenty-year-old son who was learning English at the university. I concluded that they must not ticket many foreigners in Komsomolsk, as I had to go back and forth between two offices a couple of times in order to get a ticket. Only four days in Russia, and I was already feeling frustrated with not understanding the language. With the ticket issue finally settled, we boarded the train and settled into our compartments. So on the evening of August 8, I departed Komsomolsk on the seven-and-a-half-hour trip to Visakogorny, which is the nearest community to Siziman Bay.

About two hours out of Komsomolsk, the train pulled into the small village of Selikhino. I noticed a number of people, mostly older women and young kids, were lined up along the station platform. Various vegetables, fish, berries, bread, and other items were displayed for passengers to purchase—some on small tables or boxes, others simply spread out on blankets before the sellers. When the train stopped, Andrei grabbed his passport, jumped up, and was soon outside, walking back and forth among the other passengers acquiring food items for the remainder of the trip. It was interesting, but it appeared that no one went anywhere without their passport documentation. The stopover was relatively brief, and soon after leaving Selikhino, Andrei proceeded to set up dinner. The table fare for the evening consisted of sausage, tomatoes, cucumbers, cheese, bread, mineral water, and vodka. This was to be my first, but definitely not my last exposure to Russian traditions. Since I was not a big fan of tomatoes or cucumbers, at the time I stuck with the sausage, cheese, and bread. My attitude toward the vodka was *What the hell.*

The weather had been absolutely beautiful every day since I'd been in Russia, and this evening was no different. As the train rattled on through the countryside, I was again struck with its similarity to that of the region near Fairbanks, Alaska. Gentle, rolling hills were covered with birch, aspen, and spruce forests; few signs of civilization, and mostly open space. Even though I did not really know what we were toasting, in short order we downed three shots. With the sudden rush of alcohol going to my head and considering that we were traveling at night, it did not take me too long to fall asleep to the rocking and rhythmic *cha-chunk, cha-chunk, cha-chunk* of the railcar.

A remote village of less than three thousand people, Visakogorny is situated in a small valley up in the northern Sikhote Alin Mountains. During the 1940s and into the '50s, the area was the site of a Japanese POW camp and existed primarily for the construction of this portion of the BAM railroad. "Visakogorny" translates as "high mountain valley," and from what I was told, it was at one time referred to as "the valley of the dead." We arrived at about 2:30 a.m. and were met by Lydia Nikoliavich, a local woman who served as expeditor for the Siziman Bay operations. Lydia was a pleasant lady. She appeared to be in her mid-forties, about 5 feet 2 inches tall with short blonde hair, a pleasingly plump figure, and large breasts. My gear filled up the small car that came to pick us up, so we had to walk to the company-owned apartment where we were to spend the rest of the night.

Arriving in total darkness at an apartment building that had certainly seen its better days, we—or rather, I—stumbled into the apartment, ready for more sleep. The tiny apartment was dirty and had one bedroom, a living room, kitchen, and bathroom. In order to flush the toilet you had to empty a bucket of water into it. I was soon ushered into the kitchen where again the sausage, tomatoes, cucumbers, bread, mineral water, and vodka were placed onto the table. While Andrei, Lydia, and a couple of other guys conversed about who knows what, I sat quietly just watching their interaction. Andrei was a nice guy and tried his best to communicate with me. Eventually I pulled out a recent issue of *Salmon Trout Steelheader* and everyone quickly became fascinated with the pictures of fish, scenery, and even the equipment advertisements in it. Finding some common ground, so to speak, I learned one of my first Russian words, *rebalkan*, which means fishing. My shot glass was refilled, a toast to *rebalkan* was made, and we downed another drink. Eventually, after a half dozen shots of vodka, I wandered out into the living room and laid down on an old worn-out sofa. I awoke later that morning to the sound of the others hustling around, getting prepared to leave for camp.

The road to Siziman Bay was roughly 140 kilometers and took about ten hours to drive. The first half of the road was in relatively good shape—gravel, but fairly well maintained due to it being the primary access route for one of the nearby logging operations. After driving about eighty kilometers, we stopped at the bridge crossing the Tumnin River, a large river flowing through what essentially was a wilderness region. Standing on the bridge, with the only sound being that of the pristine water passing under me, I immediately thought of salmon fishing. What amazing looking country this area was, reminding me of parts of the Yukon Territory in northern Canada. In all directions were hillsides covered with mature spruce and larch forests. Occasionally an area of younger vegetation could be seen, rejuvenating entire hillsides, bringing life back to the forest following an old wildfire.

While at the river, we had lunch which consisted of, you guessed it, sausage, cheese, tomatoes, cucumbers, bread, mineral water, and of course, vodka. After finishing lunch, the five of us climbed back up into the truck and continued our journey. Twenty-five kilometers or so after the Tumnin River, the road condition drastically deteriorated. We came to a stretch of road—and I use the term "road" loosely—which was nothing more than a trail over a boulder-strewn hillside. This was immediately followed by a stretch of road covered by water that was overflowing from the nearby river. Upon arriving at the bridge crossing on the Chichimara River, we stopped and everyone climbed out of the truck.

Crossing the Chichimara River

Standing at the edge of the bridge, I wondered how we would make the crossing to the other side. The midspan support of the log stringer bridge had apparently been undermined by the high waters during the spring runoff. The result was that two-thirds of the bridge now had two to three feet of water flowing over it. To the Russians, the solution to this problem was a simple one. We, along with all our gear and camp supplies, were transferred into what amounted to a tank without the gun turret. This track vehicle then carefully straddled what was left of the bridge and cautiously transported us to a crew truck waiting on the other side. Nearing Siziman Bay, we came to a stretch of road that was still under construction. Here the driver eased the truck onto the log sub-base which would eventually serve to "float" the rock surfacing of the completed road across the muskeg-type soil, and we slowly bounced along. When the logs ran out, we were hooked onto a TT-4 track machine and were towed through the axle-high muck until we hit gravel road once again. It was here, along this stretch of road, that I saw my first of two Asiatic Black Bears. Coming over the pass, the road quickly dropped in elevation through a series of sharp curves (referred to as the "serpentine") and into the spruce forest of the Siziman River valley.

Finally, six days after leaving the States, I arrived at the camp at Siziman Bay early in the evening on the ninth. I was taken to what was affectionately referred to as the "Gulag," an ATCO complex which was brought in from Canada for the expats to live in. This was going to be home, and I was glad to have finally arrived. As I opened up the door, I heard someone shouting, "Where in the hell is this fucking Forest Service expert know-it-all that has come to tell us all how to do it right?" I introduced myself, and then told this old fart standing in front of me not to ever insult me again by referring to me as someone from the Forest Service. Shaking his hand and chuckling, I then asked, "Just who in the hell are you?" He introduced himself as Joe Dill, a log scaler from Alaska who had been in Siziman Bay for about two months. Joe and I immediately hit it off and subsequently formed a lasting friendship that would help get us through the ordeals of life at Siziman Bay.

Joe led me to one of the twenty-five bedrooms, and we set my baggage inside the small six-foot by ten-foot room. He then gave me a quick rundown on the bathroom facility which was equipped with four showers, four toilets, and a row of sinks. "You're lucky," he said. "Up until a couple of weeks ago, the water and sewer weren't hooked up, and we had to use one of the Russian outhouses down on the other side of camp." Joe then left to head down to the log yard while I commenced to unpack and settle in. The room came furnished with a small single bed, clothes cabinet with two dresser drawers, a small desk, and a chair. Nothing fancy, but comfortable enough and I thought, *What more does a cast-aside, middle-aged, soon-to-be-divorced guy really need?*

Later that evening, I was brought down to meet Nikolay Potarov, the Russian General Manager for the Siziman Bay operations. Potarov's room was in one of the eight standard, blue Russian prefab-style buildings used for offices and/or sleeping quarters. A silver-gray-haired man standing about five feet ten inches tall, he was, other than a belly that hung over his jeans, of stout stature. His eyes were bloodshot, and his face had a reddish hue to it—a clear sign of too much alcohol. When he smiled, which he did often, his gold tooth would shine brightly in the light. He also had a handshake grip that could shatter your fingers.

Following a short introductory discussion, we went to another room which was the sleeping quarters for two of the women log scalers. It was here that the welcome party really started. A small table was prepared with various salads, sausages, bread, mineral water, juice, vodka, and champagne. Maybe it was because I had not had anything other than sausage, cheese, and bread for the past two days, but I found the salads a very welcome fare. When I say "salads," I do not mean the type of salads you might get with dinner back in the States. There was calamari mixed with egg and mayonnaise, wild fern with oil and ground pork, potato cubes with pickle, peas and sausage chunks, and beets with mayonnaise.

The welcoming party included Natasha (the Chief Scaler) whom we later nicknamed Big Red due to her hair color and being the oldest of three Natashas at camp. Lena, whose mother was Lydia back in Visakogorny, was a young girl with wavy dark hair and dark brown "bedroom eyes." Her full lips were the kind that movie stars back in Hollywood paid big bucks to some overrated plastic surgeon to obtain. Reema was an older-looking woman, probably only in her forties, but who reminded me of my grandmother. Olga was a good-looking young, blue-eyed blonde, well-endowed, but "blind as a bat" woman from Kodiak, one of the smaller villages along the rail near Visakogorny. Gennady, a well-educated, soft-spoken young man from Khabarovsk who spoke fluent Russian, English, and Chinese, served as one of our translators. Before the first toast, Jack Navell, one of the expats, told me that the trick was to continuously eat, "Otherwise the vodka will floor you." So, since I was extremely hungry anyway, eat I did—and dance. Once the girls learned that I liked to dance, I could hardly sit down the rest of the evening.

About midnight, I staggered back through camp up to my room in the Gulag. Immediately upon laying down on my bed, the world started to rapidly spin. Not having anything else available, I ripped the pillowcase off my pillow and puked my guts out. I think that not only did I lose everything I had eaten that evening, but quite possibly everything from the past two or three days. I'm not sure that there is anything much worse to smell than the mixture of regurgitated vodka, potato, and cucumber. I learned later on that this was referred to as the true Russian "salute."

When I finally was able to get to my feet, I opened the window, fell back on my bed, and didn't wake until around 10:00 a.m. the next morning. Fortunately, no one else was in the Gulag, having long since gone to work. I quickly took my bed sheets, pillowcase, and shirt outside, and with a garden hose rinsed off all the vomit that I could. Then after placing my things in the washing machine, I headed for the bathroom to take a long shower. The Gulag's "kitchen" was nothing more than a converted bedroom and contained a microwave, small refrigerator, small table, and three chairs. While sitting in the kitchen drinking coffee and slowly coming back to life, Jack came in to congratulate me on being accepted by the Russians. "You passed the test," he commented. He went on to say that my ability to hold my vodka had apparently impressed them. Age, education, and experience were respected, but a man's worth was to some extent still measured by the amount of vodka he could drink. To this day, no one at camp knows just how bad of shape I was in that night.

Chapter Two

Learning the Ropes

B efore lunch, I took a ride with Jack out to the logging operations to check out the type of equipment being used, the logging practices, roads, etc. My stomach was still in turmoil, and we had to make several "emergency" stops on the way. I told Jack that I thought it was something I had eaten on the way into camp the previous day. When I returned to camp, I opted out of having lunch and instead took a short nap so that I would hopefully feel better afterward. Later that afternoon, I wandered down to the log yard to see what was going on.

The logs were neatly bundled and stacked in rows. At the log scaling area, a Caterpillar 980F Front-end Log Loader was unloading the trucks as they arrived and placing the logs onto two roll-out skids. Here, two women scalers would measure log diameters, grade, and mark the logs. A third scaler would keep record of the daily production. A Caterpillar 325 Log Loader sorted the logs into various steel racks according to species, length, and quality sort. When the rack was full, the logs were taken to the appropriate log deck by another Caterpillar 980F. I found Joe sitting in the "scale shack" drinking tea with Big Red. Actually, I found him lying down on the bench with a big smile on his face, his head on Natasha's lap as she gave him a facial massage. At this point I should have realized that life at Siziman Bay was going to be like nothing I could have ever imagined.

Joe walked back through the log yard with me, explaining what he knew about the operations as we went. All the logs were banded with wire into neatly uniform bundles with the exception of those in two decks situated off in the far corner of the log yard. I asked Joe why these logs were separate from the others and was informed that they were *dravah*, which is Russian for "firewood." Apparently these logs were not of good enough quality to be suitable for export.

I walked around one of the log decks then commented, "You're messing with me aren't you?" Joe replied, "No, according to their Russian GOST [Government Official Standard Technology] these logs have too much defect to even be pulp quality." "Joe, I've sent worse-looking logs than these to the pulp mills back in the States and never had an issue." Joe chuckled and commented, "I know, I've seen the same in Alaska."

I shook my head in disbelief as we walked away. At that point I wanted to see where and how we were going to load the logs onto ships, so I asked Joe if he'd walk down to the jetty with me. The short five-minute walk took us past a log cabin which enclosed the laundry room and *banya* (sauna). About midway along the road was the generator building holding two Caterpillar diesel generators and an area containing the fuel storage tanks.

The jetty had been designed and its construction overseen by a company from Finland. Located a few hundred feet from the mouth of the Siziman River, it was not much more than a lot of rock dumped into the bay forming a platform from which to ship. In excess of $7 million, it was immediately obvious to me that the facility was poorly designed and cost too much. From what I was told, apparently Frontier had already invested in excess of $20 million into the Siziman Bay project. With production at extremely poor levels and no logs being sold or shipped as of yet, frustration among the US partners was high.

Not too far upstream, and within tidal influence was an old fish-processing camp. Two of the weathered gray buildings extended slightly out over the river. For the most part, these buildings had been abandoned and nothing of any use or value remained. A third smaller building situated behind these two appeared to be a combination of living quarters and banya. Apparently this building was still being used on occasion by the few fishermen tending their nets along the beach.

I had been in camp only one day but could already sense the tension between the Americans and Russians. It was clear to see that the higher-level management personnel, both American and Russian, hated each other, and as a result there was only limited cooperation—if any—between them. Ron Pritchard, the American General Manager, outwardly showed his dislike for the Russians and treated them with zero respect. During the standard evening meeting held to discuss the day's results, decide on the night shift's activities, and plan for the next day, Ron disagreed with almost everything. He continually cussed and swore profanity at the Russian managers, telling them how stupid they were.

Following the meeting, Andrei was so mad that he took me aside, and with Genady translating, told me that if we did not do the logging his way, I would not be there next year. I thought to myself, *This is an easy threat since my time here in Russia is by invitation only.* But I was embarrassed by Ron's actions and could not blame the Russians for being upset. I assured Andrei that I did not appreciate Ron's attitude and that it was not my style. I was able to calm him down, and then asked if I could go to the woods with him in the morning. I wanted to "pick his brain" to learn how he identifies areas for harvest, designs roads and logging units, etc. He agreed to do so and went off to have dinner. With my head still aching, I went back to the Gulag to get some sleep.

It was raining when I woke up the next day, so hard at times it felt like Southeast Alaska. My headache was gone, but I was still unsure about my stomach. I was hungry though, so I decided to have breakfast, which was something like Cream of Wheat and a simple bread roll. I finished quickly and was looking forward to going out into the forest with Andrei and Genady. Unfortunately, I hadn't realized that Ron planned on going with us, and when Andrei found out he went ballistic! He said he would be happy to go with me but not Ron. I took him off to the side and was able to calm him down once again. "Andrei," I said, "if this one time you would do this for me, I would really appreciate it. Just let Ron come with us and don't create a problem for me." He reluctantly agreed, and we hopped into the Russian UAZ, which was similar in appearance to the older style Toyota Land Cruiser, and took off up the road. Maybe it was just one old forester to another, but I liked Andrei, and I believe he liked me as well.

On the way out, we talked about the various forest animals found in the Russian Far East, the Pacific Northwest, and Alaska. We also discussed hunting and guns. Andrei commented that although he had never seen an actual one, he liked the Winchester lever action rifle. His only exposure to this rifle was from having seen it in an old Yul Brynner movie, *The Magnificent Seven*. He was excited and impressed to learn that I actually owned one. During the trip, Ron continuously made fun of Andrei and his comments. Fortunately Genady had the common sense not to translate most of what was being said. Andrei could not have cared less about what Ron was saying, choosing instead to completely ignore him. We wandered around in the woods for about two hours, and at one point I stepped onto a hornets nest. Although I was not in as good of physical condition as Andrei was nor as quick, I was faster than Ron who ended up being the only one nailed by the angry little buggers.

I asked Andrei about aerial photography, and I was surprised to hear that this was not available to use. I thought to myself that if I could ever get some satellite photos of the area I could not only show him what a valuable tool it was, but be able to redirect his enormous energy toward more productive fieldwork. I just figured it would take some time, patience, and keeping Ron out of it.

Later that evening after dinner, I spent three hours in the office trying to fix the satellite telephone that Ron somehow screwed up. I couldn't believe it. Here was a $21,000 piece of equipment, and Ron in his frustration and anger starts banging on it, how stupid can a guy be!

Breakfast the next morning was the same Cream of Wheat-type cereal as the previous day. I quickly learned to keep an eye out for and eat around the black chunks of rocks in it, but other than that it tasted okay. Usually I had to head for the bathroom within fifteen to twenty minutes though, as none of the food provided in the camp kitchen had any real substance to it and tended to go right through the digestive system.

The Author

I accompanied Andrei out to the woods again, this time without Ron. It turned out to be a very productive and informative day for me. Continually asking questions, I learned as much as I could about what the Russians were required to do, would like to do, and what they were thinking of doing at Siziman Bay. Initially I thought we were just randomly walking through the forest. However, we suddenly came upon a narrow corridor cut through the trees. Andrei began to look for a blazed tree or post marked with handwritten descriptions. Once located, we followed the path until we came to a corner, then followed the other path in the new direction. I soon realized that these were some sort of survey lines. When I questioned Andrei about them, he informed me that some of these were for "Quartile" boundary locations while others were "vision lines." Quartiles are basically land subdivisions similar to Townships or Sections used in the United States. Vision lines were exactly what they sound like—paths cut through the forest in order for the Russian foresters to walk out into an area and "see" what the timber was like. Apparently Andrei had recently hired a couple of Inventory Foresters to do this surveying and assist in identifying potential harvest areas.

During the next couple of days, I continued to go into the forest with Andrei. On one of these days, we stopped a short distance from camp and went to where the Inventory Foresters had set up their base. Located along the Siziman River, I took advantage to try some fishing while the Russians discussed business. When I returned, Andrei offered to show me a couple of high elevation infrared aerial photographs of the Siziman Bay area that the foresters had. I was surprised, since previously I was told that the military was the only agency with access to this resource.

Apparently these foresters obtained this set through something other than proper channels. They requested numerous times that I keep the existence of these photographs a secret from the other Russians, especially the camp security guard who happened to be ex-KGB. Andrei and the two foresters were truly terrified about this, and I promised not to tell anyone. I would have liked to have taken the photos back to camp and made copies of them. However, even if Andrei would have agreed, they were too large to process through our fax machine which unfortunately was also the copier. I was quickly coming to understand that the Russian foresters were not stupid, as Ron would have others believe. It appeared to me that the main issue was more that their technology had basically stopped at the beginning of the Cold War following World War II.

During these ventures into the woods, Genady would overload my brain by constantly explaining the Russian words for the various plants and animals found in the region. While crossing a small stream, I noticed a couple of bear tracks in the sand. Supposedly from an Asiatic Black Bear, the prints were similar in size to those of a grizzly bear in Interior Alaska. Genady also explained why foresters in Russia got paid so little. According to him, the Russian Czar, Peter the Great, considered the forests a dark and mysterious place and those who worked there, devious people. "As such, he paid the foresters minimal wages, figuring that they would just steal the rest that they required to live." I don't know if this story is true, but it made sense. I had always told my ex-wife that she would never get rich being married to a forester.

I kept bugging Andrei about the photos throughout the week. I told him that if I could just have them for a day I could prepare a map identifying potential harvest areas and a conceptual road plan. One afternoon, Andrei came into my office, closed the door behind him, and laid the two infrared aerial photographs on my desk. He told me *"dvah dehn"* (two days), and placing his finger to his lips, signaled me to be quiet about this and then left. I was in shock that he apparently trusted me to this extent, but was extremely pleased and quickly began to work on an operating plan.

About this time, a new poodle-type dog arrived in camp, adding to the bunch of five or six mangy-looking mixed-breed ones that were already running around the place. We also acquired a new

Russian Log Yard Boss who had come in with the crew change on the fifteenth. Ivan Karlikoff was a short, cocky guy with bushy gray hair that reminded me of Art Garfunkel's style. First thing in the morning, he and I got into an argument on log yard operations. "This is Russia," he shouted at me, "you don't know anything about loading ships or what is required!" "Don't insult my intelligence," I responded. "You can either work with me on yard operations, or I can ignore your suggestions." With that said, Ivan walked away shouting something else back at me that Misha didn't want to translate—but I got the point. I had already determined that, at least initially, my influence on changing the timber harvest operations would be limited. Subsequently I decided that the log yard procedures and ship loading activities were where I would force my authority. This, I felt, was where I would be able to make the biggest impact on the efficiency and profitability of the operation.

Old Gulag Cabin

A week later, I hiked up what was referred to as Gulag Creek in an attempt to identify a possible road location to take us over the mountains to the south of camp. Along the way, I came upon a half dozen old log cabins nestled within a stand of birch trees. It was a haunting sign of when the Russian prisoner camp was in operation here from 1941 to 1953. I had been told that under Stalin's rule, an estimated twenty-to thirty-thousand prisoners died at Siziman Bay during this time period. Two of these cabins were about 2½ kilometers up the creek, and even the Russians were not aware of their existence. Further on up the valley, I saw my first sable, a mink like animal with a face similar to that of a cat. There was a fair amount of sign that moose frequented the area as well—and ticks! I picked four of the little fellas off me during this excursion, one of them as it was beginning to dig into my stomach. Lord, how I hated those things! On the drive back to camp, I saw three Grey Herons roosting in a tall larch tree alongside the road near a small creek. Obviously extremely wary of people, they immediately took to flight when I stopped the vehicle to take some pictures.

I went down to the Siziman River before dinner to try for some salmon, and although I didn't catch anything, I did have one bite. The Pink Salmon were well past their prime, but I believed the Coho run was just beginning to come on. Unfortunately, the Russians had the entire beach lined with their damn nets, so I wasn't sure I would ever be able to catch a fish. Even if I did catch a salmon, I had decided that I would release it and let it try to survive the rest of its journey upriver to spawn. It was hard for me to believe that any group of people could overfish a river system with their nets any worse than the Indians back in Washington State, but these guys seemed to be doing it. On top of this, there were about a dozen seals off the mouth of the river also taking their toll on the salmon population. On the way back to camp, I stopped to watch a couple of Russians with small dip nets wading in the bay trying to catch shrimp. Not the most efficient way of doing it, but they were able to catch a few here and there.

Dinner really sucked that evening. The mashed potatoes were so runny that you had to use a spoon to eat them. We also had what can best be described as a fish mash having the consistency of tuna fish sandwich spread. I commented to Hubert that "as Crocodile Dundee said, 'It'll fill you, but it tastes like shit.'" I filled myself up on buttered bread while wondering if this was what it was like for the prisoners in the original camp.

August 24th was a beautiful autumn day, sunny, cool in the morning and warm in the afternoon. There was nothing real pressing, so I knocked off work at 5:30 p.m. I sat outside the Gulag with a couple of the young translators, Vladislav (*Slava*) and Mikhail (*Misha*), listening to Credence Clearwater Revival booming on my stereo. We enjoyed "grooving" to the music while the both of them tried to help me learn some Russian. At 7:00 p.m., we headed down to the kitchen for dinner, which sucked even more than the usual. The usual mashed potatoes were there, but this night we had some kind of mystery meat patty that even Misha couldn't place the taste of.

Throughout the summer, the Russian carpenters had been laboriously constructing a huge building for a shop facility where maintenance work on the logging equipment could be performed. The last wall was finally completed just prior to the September 1st crew change. With the lower half of the walls constructed from spruce logs, the facility became sarcastically referred to as Fort Apache. Unfortunately, it appeared that no one thought of measuring the size of the equipment we use, and both doors were too small for half of the machinery we had. On the other hand, one of these carpenters made me a beautiful office chair out of some scrap lumber. It looked like something you would put out on your back porch or lawn, but at least it was comfortable, and I finally had something to sit on at my desk other than a chunk of firewood.

Dinner that night was really *dehrmo*, a Russian word which roughly translates as "shit." I was able to eat the mashed potatoes, but I took one bite of the shredded carrots and scraped them aside. No one could figure out what the cooks had mixed in with them. I just couldn't believe they were able to screw up cooking carrots. The mystery meat smelled like fish and even had a touch of rotten-fish flavor to it, but I guess it was some kind of meat patty. Once again I was fortunate that there was plenty of freshly baked bread and butter on the table that I could fill up on.

Morale among the Russian crew seemed to be getting increasingly worse. Their pay was low when compared to other known logging operations, averaging only 1,300,000 rubles (roughly $295 US) per month. On top of this, the pay was usually late, and the poor folks were charged $90 per month for the lousy meals they were served there at camp. The Russian Management back in Komsomolsk had the attitude that "if they don't like it, let them quit." The problem with this concept was that the people who did stay on were in general worthless and probably couldn't get a job anywhere else. They tended to care less about what they were doing, the result being that we got poor quality, low production, and no preventative maintenance on the equipment. The exceptions to this rule were the people working in the sort yard and camp operations.

I woke up the next morning to another beautiful, albeit cold, fall morning. After numerous discussions, last night I finally won my battle with one of the Russian electricians. I finally got him to understand how the furnace worked and that with the thermostat set at sixty degrees, he didn't need to turn the stupid thing off at night! Subsequently it felt good to wake up in a reasonably warm room. Since it was Sunday and the weather was so nice, I took a couple of hours off midday and again tried fishing for salmon down at the mouth of the Siziman River. I didn't catch anything, not even a bite, but I did see four skuzzy-looking spawned-out humpies. I returned to camp, extremely disappointed with the lack of salmon in the river, which I figured was due to continued overfishing of the resource and a declining fish population.

While back in the office, I sat and listened to Ron in one of his heated discussions with Potarov and some other managers in the room next door. It was always embarrassing for me listening to Ron with his "God damn this" and "fuck that" language that he used when dealing with or talking about the Russians. The Russians had some problems and certainly were not 100 percent cooperative, but I felt that this was significantly in part due to Ron himself.

Later, I overheard a couple of the crew telling Potarov that they saw and killed a snake with a "diamond-shaped head" down by the jetty. Unfortunately it fell back into the rocks, so they were unable to retrieve it. When I asked Misha why all the fuss, he said that according to the Russians, this type of snake was poisonous. I don't know if this was really true, but it did make a person think twice about climbing around the rocks down at the beach.

After dinner, I spent almost two hours in the office explaining to Gregorie Dudnikoff, one of the Russian foresters, that a harvest unit did not have to be square. It was frustrating, but I finally got him to understand that the hectares (acreage) could be determined even if there were more than four, six, or even eight angles to the unit. It's just amazing to think that these foresters had been working for more than twenty years and now was the first time they had had aerial photographs to use. Unfortunately, the problem was that they did not understand what they were really looking at and how to effectively use these photographs to minimize their time wandering around out in the woods. Even more amazing was that this was also the first time that they had topographic maps available as well. I can't imagine any forester back in the United States having to design roads and/or harvest units without the use of aerial photos, let alone topographic maps. I came out of the meeting with a different appreciation of these folks and what they had been able to accomplish with little or no resources at their disposal.

About one week later, I was looking for Jack so I could hitch a ride with him up to the logging sites. Nobody had seen him since the previous evening, and it was unusual for him not to be around for our morning coffee bullshit sessions. After lunch, I headed up to the Gulag and noticed Jack's pickup parked out front. When I was close enough, I could see him sitting behind the steering wheel sleeping. I banged on the door to wake him up, and he showed no movement. Jack remained motionless as I banged even harder. *Oh shit*, I thought, *the dumb bastard drank himself to death*. I went to the door of the Gulag and hollered for some help, not wanting to deal with this by myself. However, no one else was around to help, so I opened the door to the pickup and tried again to wake him up. He wasn't dead, but at one in the afternoon he was still drunk beyond comprehension. I looked at him and wondered how he even was able to drive himself back to the Gulag. Since this truck was one of two which the expats had available for use, I pulled him from the truck to take him to his room; however, his limp body was too heavy and unmanageable for me to handle, and he crumpled to the ground. "The hell with you, Jack," I mumbled. "I don't have time to deal with this now." Shaking my head in disgust, I stepped over him and into the truck. I left him lying on the ground to sleep it off and drove down to the office to pick up my gear. Shortly after this incident, Jack left Siziman Bay, and the last I heard, he had accepted a job with some company in Southeast Asia.

Our Log Sales Representative in Japan had said no, however, the Russian Management in Komsomolsk was telling us that a ship was scheduled to arrive in two days. Although I did not believe a vessel was coming, after one week of suggesting we do a practice run, I convinced the Russian managers to begin transferring logs down to the jetty in preparation for the ship's arrival. I also wanted to test the entire ship loading procedure that had been agreed to.

Immediately, Karlikoff got the sort yard crew all upset and confused. When I approached him to discuss the situation, he again informed me, through our interpreter Genady, that I was stupid. "The procedure you have for loading the ship is stupid," he continued, "and if you don't change and do it my way, I will not accept any responsibility!" "Ivan," I replied, "I don't care if you accept responsibility or not, and this is the second time now that you have insulted me. I have never insulted you, so why do you feel you need to do so to me?"

He continued to argue, and I finally said, "Look, the loading procedure we are following was discussed and agreed upon with Potarov and Vladislav Shukalov." His quick response to this was, "I don't care; it is stupid and wrong." "Ivan," I replied, "I appreciate that you have a difference of opinion, but you should care since they are your superiors. We are going to proceed as planned." I also told him that if I was wrong, I would come apologize, but if I was right, I would expect him to apologize to me! It was difficult at times for me not to laugh at Ivan, for he tried so hard to be boss. But I found it quite comical that this man, who stood no taller than four feet eight inches, had a last name which essentially translates as "Little Dwarf."

The loading of logs onto the trucks in the sort yard and their subsequent unloading with the crane on the jetty was not smooth by any means. Although certainly not sufficient to load a ship in a timely manner, we did learn where our problems were. In the morning, I had requested two log trucks for the operation, but Potarov had insisted that one would be sufficient. Not wanting to argue, I reluctantly agreed. However, Potarov also agreed that if the one truck was not enough, he would give me two. By noon I had three trucks moving logs to the jetty. It was September 1st, and this unfortunately meant it was the day for crew shift change. Most of the crew was drunk when they arrived. The drinking continued throughout the day and into the evening, so to get any Russian who not only could work but would, was an accomplishment in itself.

Later that evening Sergei, one of the electricians, came crawling into the Gulag. Joe saw him first, and thinking that he had hurt himself somehow, called out for someone to get the doctor and Potarov. At the time, we did not know that he was drunk out of his gourd. Potarov showed up first and immediately threw a fit. He picked Sergei up off the floor and threw him through the doorway into his bedroom—or at least he tried to. The poor guy's left leg hit the door framing on the way through, causing it to snap. Sergei laid on the floor in a fetal position as Potarov continued to scream at him while literally smacking the hell out of him. When the doctor finally showed up and informed us of Sergei's condition, Potarov refused to let him be treated. Instead, Sergei had to crawl around camp for the next two days before Potarov calmed down enough to allow the doctor to reset his leg and send him back to Visakogorny. This was the first and last time that I ever saw Sergei drink in camp.

The transfer of logs to the jetty continued to improve throughout the next day. The Russians even started to think of ways to speed things up and were coming to me with their suggestions. We still had a lot of room for improvement, but I was pleased that they were working with me and thinking rather than just doing what they were told.

A small fishing vessel stopped by the jetty this morning. While there, they proudly showed me the huge head and blood-soaked hide of a wild boar they apparently shot just north of Siziman. I found this interesting, since I was unaware that wild pigs lived in this region. Misha was also surprised to learn of this. A couple of the Russian crew members got some squid from the fishermen and invited me to the scalers' shack for a midday snack. The girls fried up some of the squid and boiled the rest for this unexpected but greatly appreciated treat. Unfortunately, at breakfast the next morning, I learned that the "wild boar" was actually Antoine's pet hog that had been taken by the fisherman. He was considerably depressed about it when I saw him.

Karlikoff wrote up a formal complaint letter to Potarov accusing me of violating Russian safety codes during the third day of log transfer operations, including "decking logs while it was raining." What bullshit! If you couldn't do any work in the rain, then how in the hell would you ever get anything accomplished in this region? He also hated that while checking sort quality, I would climb up on top of the log decks, which apparently is also against code. I now had to write a formal response to the pain-in-the-ass little shit's accusations. Frustrating, I would go out of my way to be friendly and try to work with him, but he just refused. The only consolation I had in this regard was that he was that way with everyone, including the Russians. I did kind of feel a little sorry for the guy though, since he was not liked by anyone in camp.

While monitoring how the operation was going, I walked into the scalers' shack to get an update on the volume trucked to the jetty and to learn more on how they were accounting for this. Reema was busy cooking up a couple of dozen trout that one of the guys had brought in. The smell of flour-coated fish frying in a well-oiled iron skillet over a woodstove immediately reminded me of camping in the Olympic Mountains of Washington when I was a kid. Since I had skipped breakfast, I agreed without hesitation to their invitation to join them once again for another midday snack. Cooked in a simple fashion, the trout tasted wonderful, and although I didn't understand what was being said, it was interesting to watch the jovial interactions of these people. I had only been at Siziman Bay for a few weeks, but I was really beginning to like the Russians. It would amaze me that despite the often miserable living conditions they endure, they had a tendency to joke a lot and thoroughly enjoy each other's company.

A storm blew in on the evening of September 4th and continued throughout the entire next day. The waves in the bay were about three feet high, and at high tide they would break over the jetty. Portions of the rock surfacing on the dock itself were being washed away, and every wave breaking up against it would cause water to spew up like a geyser. One of the channel buoys was washed ashore, and the two others moved out of place. I hadn't seen a storm like this since I was at Icy Bay along the Gulf of Alaska.

Midmorning, as the storm continued to rage on, I was sitting alone in the cramped room we were forced to use as a kitchen-lounge area contemplating what to do on such a wet miserable morning. Soon my frustration with not having an adequate lounge area for the expats to use overtook me. I grabbed a hammer and proceeded to tear off the panels on the wall separating the kitchen area from the vacant room next door. Igor, one of the Russian handymen, had heard the noise and was soon standing at the door watching me. He left and shortly returned with a crowbar and Skil saw. Not being able to speak English, he motioned his desire to help me out. Well over six feet tall with a mouth full of silver false teeth, Igor always reminded me of the James Bond character Jaws. I replied, "*Neyht problem*," and in short order we were down to only the studs. Igor cut the 2x4's out, and we now had doubled the size of the kitchen lounge. Among other things, Igor turned out to be a skilled electrician, and in short order took care of the wiring that we had exposed. The other expats came in after lunch, and we all spent the rest of the day remodeling the room and rearranging furniture. When finished, we celebrated by having coffee and some pastries I got from the cook down in the kitchen.

Misha came into the Gulag and told me "it was true." Sharkoff, apparently without our consultation and in conflict with our marketing agreement with Shasta Corporation, had chartered a vessel for a shipment of pulp logs. It was scheduled to arrive the next day. Unfortunately, by the end of the day, roughly fifty feet along the south side of the access road had been washed away, making it impassable for log trucks. The Russians quickly attached a "clam" bucket to the crane and began to pull the large rip-rap boulders back in against the road bed. When the *M/V Georgi Shabzhukhov* arrived, repair work was sufficiently completed to enable loading operations to begin.

While ship loading activities were going on, I decided to take a quick trip out to the harvest areas and check on what was happening. On the way out, I discovered one of the reasons why our daily production was low. One of the Freightliner log trucks was parked near a small creek, and the driver was carrying a bucket of water to wash down the cab. Even though loaded with logs, this thirty-minute-plus routine was apparently standard procedure on each trip back to the log yard. I was happy to see that the truck drivers took some pride in the appearance of these trucks; however, this delay in deliveries had to stop. I instructed this driver, and subsequently all the others, that the washing of trucks was to be limited to once a day, and only on their last trip in from the woods.

We had recently received, and were in the process of installing two new Caterpillar diesel generators which would enable us to increase the electrical capacity at camp. That afternoon I decided to go down to the generator building and check on the progress being made. As I approached the building, I could hear a steady humming sound. I thought this rather strange since the generators were not yet hooked up to the system. Upon opening the door, the place exploded with hundreds of flies. I say hundreds, but it was probably more like thousands. Apparently some of the Russians had chosen this building as a location to hang their salmon to air-dry, probably thinking that the closed facility would be safe from this type of infestation. How wrong they were. I walked around the facility, holding my hand over my nose and mouth, and thinking *Well, at least I know not to accept any offer of dried salmon while here at camp.*

The sunrises during late September at Siziman Bay were some of the most beautiful that I have ever seen. Often I would wake up in the morning before daylight, grab a cup of coffee, and head down to the beach to watch the beginning of a new day. A variety of seabirds was always there, and sometimes seals would be lying out on the reef. I'd sit on the rocks, listening to the sounds around me before the rest of the camp woke up, and watch the sun come up in all its glory. One morning as the brilliant red-orange sun came up over the horizon, I could understand perhaps why the Japanese had decided to use this as their national symbol. For me, however, these morning sunrises were God's promise that no matter how crazy, frustrating, or bad the day before was, it was past and just didn't matter anymore. Here was His promise of a new day, a new start with a clean slate, and it gave me the strength to continue on—a calming, cleansing of the soul so to speak.

Our second vessel of the season, the *M/V Sibirskiy 2117* arrived on September 16th, this time for a load of sawlogs. During the second day of loading, Joe, Hubert, and I met the captain on deck while watching the loading operations. Surprised to learn that there were Americans at Siziman Bay, he immediately invited us up to his cabin to visit and have a couple of beers. Captain Vladimir, a relatively handsome individual about six feet tall with brown eyes and dark brunette hair, appeared to be in his early forties. With him and Joe constantly cracking jokes, I hardly stopped laughing the entire time we were on board. The vessel departed for Japan four days later as the *M/V Sibirskiy 2111* motored into berth for its first of three shipments to be made before the closure of the shipping season in November.

Confrontation

Prior to Alexie Nazarkin's arrival at Siziman Bay, all of the Russians were nervously making preparations to ensure that everything would be acceptable for their "Director." It was the cleanest I had ever seen the camp complex. I watched from the steps of the office as the orange-and-blue M-8 helicopter circled the camp area then set down in the clearing prepared between the office and the log yard. When he stepped off of the helicopter, I could fully understand why the Russians were so nervous. Nazarkin was an impressive individual who stood about six feet two inches tall, clean shaven, and obviously extremely physically fit. He was wearing an army camouflage uniform, dark aviator-style sunglasses, and had a Makarov pistol strapped on his belt. I thought to myself, *This guy has got to be kidding*, but the next two days of events proved otherwise.

Shortly after his arrival, we all headed to the cookhouse for an elaborate lunch by all standards from that which I had seen to date. "Fresh" tomatoes and cucumbers, which I hadn't seen in over a month, a variety of sausages, and numerous bottles of vodka were placed on the tables. Two initial toasts were completed; one by Potarov and one by Pritchard, to express the mutual cooperation that existed between the Russians and Americans at Siziman Bay, and then borsht was served. The real treat for the day was that the main course consisted of beef and potatoes rather than the traditional chicken or *sasiska* (hot dog) and buckwheat that I had been required to survive on since coming to Russia. Following lunch, which included several more toasts, everyone adjourned to their rooms to, and at least in my case, sleep off the effects of over a half dozen shots of vodka and prepare for the evening meetings.

The Russians' drinking continued down at the banya, resulting in the official meetings being canceled, at least those involving the participation of any American. Later that night, screaming from somewhere outside in the complex awakened me. Shortly thereafter, there was a knock at my door and upon opening it, I found Joe with two of the women scalers, Lena and Sveta, standing there with a look of fear on their faces. The language barrier was difficult, but I was able to learn that Nazarkin was on a drunken rampage looking to bed the first woman he was able to latch on to. We figured that if Joe hid the women in his room, they would be safe.

However, Nazarkin soon appeared in the Gulag and began banging on Joe's door, shouting and demanding that the women appear. Joe finally opened his door, and with his scaling stick in hand, stood toe-to-toe, face-to-face with Nazarkin. Although he was wearing only his T-shirt and boxer shorts, Nazarkin still had the pistol strapped to his side. After a few tense minutes, with both men shouting in their respective languages that neither of the other understood, Nazarkin backed off. If Joe had not been an American, I'm sure that Nazarkin would have killed him on the spot. Before leaving the gulag, however, Nazarkin stopped at another door, shouted once, and soon departed with his son's teary-eyed fiancée in tow. I don't think I'll ever forget the look of total desperation on her face, and my feeling of complete frustration, anger, and disgust at the whole situation.

The next morning, Ron angrily told Joe and me that "this was a Russian issue, and you two should have stayed out of it." At that moment of time, I lost all remaining respect for him as a supervisor and an individual in general. Later, at a meeting directed by Nazarkin, we were instructed that "the Americans were to be put on the bus, trucked to Visakogorny, placed on the train to Khabarovsk, and never allowed to return." Fortunately, I had telephoned the office in Philadelphia earlier to inform them of the situation at hand. Knowing that I would have their full support, I stood up, told Nazarkin "we will not leave camp," then left the room. Following a rather tense day whereby the Russians attempted to ignore the Americans and vice versa, Nazarkin departed on the helicopter back to Komsomolsk, and life at Siziman Bay slowly began its transition back to a somewhat normal state. This was the first of three attempts by Nazarkin to force the Americans out of Siziman Bay.

Nobody really knew much about Nazarkin, or if they did, they were reluctant to talk about him. From what I understood though, he used to be a worker at the airplane factory in Komsomolsk. After leaving the Russian Far East for a short period of time, he somehow returned with considerable power and prestige within the Communist Party. As for me, I can honestly say that he is probably the most evil individual I have ever met. He was truly a man who, without a doubt would be able to, and probably had pulled the trigger on someone without even blinking an eye.

Not too long after the helicopter had taken off, a Russian Elkhound puppy wandered into the office. She looked so cute with the white hair of her muzzle extending up her forehead between adorable dark-brown eyes. "*Privet mylinky sabakha*" (Hi little dog), I said as she excitedly danced around in circles, her black-tipped tail wildly wagging back and forth. I couldn't resist picking her up and petting her before going back to my desk. She playfully pranced behind me, not wanting my attention to stop. I sat down, picked her up again, and as puppies will do, she immediately began to chew on my hand. Her white sock paws batted at my arm while I playfully pushed at her open mouth. Each morning after that, Sabakha, as I called her, would come into the office looking for me. Often she would follow me out into the log yard or down to the jetty.

Chapter Four

Autumn of '95

Crew Bus in Visakogorny

By the first of October, autumn had definitely arrived to this region of the Far East. I had taken the evening crew bus from camp to Visakogorny to catch the train into Khabarovsk. I woke up later in the morning as the train rolled on through a countryside filled with larch, birch, and aspen trees ablaze in their bright yellow colorations. From the looks of how people were dressed in the villages we passed through, it appeared to be windy and cold. The train pulled into Komsomolsk on schedule, and I chose to remain in my cabin during the one-hour stopover.

I was never impressed with the general appearance of this city. Although founded by "peasant settlers" in 1860, Komsomolsk basically saw its major growth following World War II. The city's center lacked any architectural diversity like that found in Khabarovsk. Dingy white and gray "*Stalinka*" and "*Kruschevka*" buildings constructed during the Cold War period dominate the area. Misha had told me that Komsomolsk was the largest manufacturing area for Russian submarines, such as the one featured in the movie *Hunt for Red October*. I understand that the city also contained a large factory producing MIG fighter jets.

My companions for the remaining trip to Khabarovsk ended up being two smelly drunks, one of whom snored exceptionally loudly. I couldn't handle the stink from these two Russians inside the small cabin, so I collected my belongings and sat out in the hallway. The train Attendant, bless her heart, was disgusted with these drunk individuals as well. Obviously feeling sorry for this poor *Amerikanski*, she placed me into a cabin with a better class of people for the remainder of the trip.

Roughly twenty-five hours after leaving camp, I finally arrived at the train station in Khabarovsk at 8:00 p.m. I was glad to see that Joe Dill was there waiting for me with a car. The driver maneuvered his well-used and abused old Lada through the mass of vehicles haphazardly parked in front of the station. I sat in the backseat thinking, *At least the steering wheel is where it's supposed to be.* Once safely—and I question the term "safely"—into the roundabout, we circled the small square at the end of Amurskaya Boulevard. At the center of the square stood a large cast-iron statue of Yerofei Khabarov, the seventeenth-century explorer for whom the city is named after. Approximately twenty feet in height, and standing atop a twenty-five-foot high granite spire, the monument towered over the surrounding area. Shortly after exiting the roundabout onto Leningradskaya Street, we passed The Cathedral of the Nativity of Christ, a rustic-looking, blue-colored, wooden Orthodox church. Two old *babushkas* (grandmas) wearing scarves stood at the front gate selling small candles and religious icons to worshipers going inside.

The driver slowly nosed the car onto Karl Marx Street then "put the pedal to the metal" before being rear-ended by another vehicle speeding its way toward the city center. He appeared to negotiate recklessly through traffic and pedestrians as we skirted Lenin Square at the intersection of Karl Marx and Muravyev-Amursky Streets. On the western edge of the large, open plaza, stood a cast-iron statue of Lenin, looking stately out over the square. A large, white five-story government administration building spanned the entire northern edge. Unlike Komsomolsk, the buildings in Khabarovsk's "center" exhibited European influence and architectural characteristics of the late 1800s to early 1900s. A variety of stores and restaurants occupied the buildings at street level; the upper floors containing either business offices or apartments.

We soon arrived at the Parus Hotel, a three-story red brick building situated near Komsomolskaya Square overlooking the Amur River. A doorman came out to meet us and assist with carrying in my baggage. In contrast to the Intourist Hotel, the city's largest with its 515 rooms, the Parus had only 11 suites, 17 rooms, one small restaurant, and a tiny bar. From what I understood, the hotel was built around the turn of the twentieth century, apparently for use by Russian dignitaries and special guests. I assumed this was why the rooms were considerably larger in size than the typical rooms found in other hotels. The entry hall at the Parus was beautifully decorated with Italian furniture and a grand piano. Marble floors added to the elegance and upscale ambiance. The rooms were very comfortable, with Italian furniture, queen-size beds, TV, desk, telephone, refrigerator, and an air-conditioning system.

The next morning was occupied with meeting our customer to discuss operations, shipments, and general market conditions in Japan. Joe and I spent half of the afternoon driving around the city, going to various stores purchasing supplies and food stuff for back at camp. At one of the public markets, Joe bought more than $500 worth of Marlboro cigarettes to give to the Russian crew for loading the last ship as quickly as they did. At the local liquor store, we purchased an ample supply of champagne, cognac, and vodka to help see us through until our next trip back to town.

That evening, I had dinner with Joe and his friends Alexander (*Sasha*) and Sasha's wife, Lena, at the Parus restaurant. After six *choot choot* shots of straight Russian vodka, which I think could have doubled as paint stripper, I developed quite a buzz. I've never seen any group of people that drank as much as the Russians. On the other hand, I've never seen any group of people with such attractive wives either! The only problem with the drinking is that the Russians don't hold their booze any better than people from other countries do, so they tend to get drunk.

By 9:00 a.m. on the morning of the fourth, Joe, Takahara, Sharkoff, and I were seated in a Russian M-8 helicopter for a flight to Siziman Bay. With a short stopover in Komsomolsk to pick up Potarov, we arrived at camp three and a half hours later. Takahara was the representative of Osika Corporation, our Japan customer that had "stepped up to the plate" and taken the time and risk to help develop markets for Siziman Bay spruce and larch production. Perhaps because he'd been involved with business in Russia for a long time, I really didn't consider Takahara to be typical Japanese. Although very serious with regard to log quality and other market-related issues, he was an extremely jovial character and a kick to be with. During this trip, he wanted to pursue the option for developing new market destinations in Japan. He felt that by producing 8.1 meter log lengths for the east coast of Japan, such as Onahama, rather than the traditional 3.8 meter and 7.6 meter produced for west coast ports, we could increase shipping options. Sharkoff listened to the proposal, then politely informed us that it could not be done—and that was the end of our discussion. Takahara of course was disappointed, but I told him I'd keep working on it.

Later that evening, Takahara, Joe, Chuck, Hubert, Misha, and I were sitting in the Gulag kitchen bullshitting and having a few drinks. In addition to saki, Takahara had also brought in some sushi and other food items from Japan which was greatly appreciated. Boris came in, and I commented to Takahara about his fondness of Credence Clearwater Revival and that he could play many of their songs on his guitar. Takahara quickly asked Boris if he would get the guitar and play for us. When he came back, Boris sat down and started to play "Bad Moon Rising," knowing that this was one of my favorites. Everyone cheered and applauded when he finished, and that started the evening of karaoke off. Boris handed Takahara the guitar, and being fluent in speaking three languages, he sang a Russian love song. I couldn't understand a word of it, but it sounded really good and Boris was impressed. Then, at Boris's request and everyone's insistence, I sang the John Denver song, "Berkley Woman." Takahara and Boris followed up with a duet.

Sharkoff heard the singing and soon appeared at the door. He stood there listening and didn't hesitate when I told him to go grab some vodka and come join us. I never could have imagined what a beautiful tenor voice he had; his singing was incredible. During the evening, it struck me what was occurring in this tiny little room in remote Far Eastern Russia. Just fifty years earlier, Russia, Japan, and the United States were at war with each other, and now, here we were sitting having drinks, singing, and enjoying each other's friendship. In fact, one of our many "toasts" of the evening was just to that.

The next day was an intense one, filled with numerous meetings, discussions, and inspections of log quality and the jetty. We discussed log sorts and quality expectations, vessel charters, market destinations in Japan, and it seemed like everything else in between.

At the end of the day, my mind was fried, and being extremely tired, I went to bed at 9:00 p.m. After two days of meetings, I finally got the Russians and Japanese to sign an agreement identifying the log sort specifications that we would base our production and subsequent shipments on. This took a major effort on my part, and believe it or not, it represented a significant leap forward in the Russians' advancement toward modernized operations. To my knowledge, at this time, Siziman Bay was the only operation in Russia that would now be providing a variety of log sorts for various different customers. It was a new concept in Russia—essentially, providing the product that the customer desired to suit specific markets.

When Sharkoff left camp the morning of the sixth, he told me that he felt he was leaving me as friends. As we watched the UAZ "Jeep" disappear as it traveled up the road, Joe commented, "You know, Dmitriy can be a real pain in the ass at times, but I kinda like the guy." "Ya," I replied "I know what you mean, but he's an all right guy. Damn Joe, it's cold this morning, feels like snow coming on. Sharkoff and Takahara flat wore me out, let's go up to the Gulag for some coffee."

I found out later in the day that it had in fact snowed up in the mountains. Another helicopter arrived shortly after lunch with Sergei Phillipov, the new President of Dalny-Les; Chekinkov; and John Cardinal, the new Vice President for Frontier. With them was the long-awaited television, VCR, and satellite dish that I had purchased prior to my leaving the States in August. Once they had settled into their rooms, I took the three of them on a walking tour of the camp, log yard, and jetty. While in the log yard, I started to get the idea that Cardinal didn't have a clue with regard to logging operations.

We were back in camp for only two days, and Joe was already halfway through the cigarettes we had purchased to give out to the crew. He could hardly walk around camp without someone coming up to him and asking for cigarettes. I doubt that Joe could remember everyone that he previously gave a pack to, and most likely some of the crew got more than their fair share.

The next day was again filled with meetings, one right after another, from just after breakfast to just before dinner. Phillipov, Chekinkov, Cardinal, Pritchard, and I discussed development of a training program for the Russian crew, the upcoming visit of representatives from the Overseas Private Investment Corporation (OPIC) coming in from the States, and the overall operations at Siziman Bay in general. Newton and Hubert got the satellite dish part of the way installed by evening. It was frustrating, although quite comical, that between Joe, myself, and three mechanics, no one could figure out how to get the damn TV and VCR working. We all read through the manuals but finally called it quits for the night, unsuccessful in our efforts.

Phillipov came into my office in the afternoon to show me his proposed schedule for the OPIC tour. This shocked the kids in the office that not only would the president of the company come to me and ask questions, but that he did so in such a gentle tone of voice and manner. I think it gave them a new appreciation of my position within the organization. The political and social class structure was still deeply imbedded within the Russian lifestyle.

I was tired of meetings and needed to head out to the forest and revive my sanity. So shortly after breakfast, Gregorie, Vadim, and I drove out to review proposed road construction and harvest units. Most of the morning was spent along Tonguska Creek discussing where to locate and then how to build a log stringer bridge. Our most significant issue was on how to place the log crib abutments. The creek, although only about fifteen feet from bank to bank, was an important coho salmon spawning and rearing stream. Gregorie just couldn't understand my insistence on not having any construction occur within the stream channel. He did, however, concede to my wishes, and we hung blue ribbon outlining the locations for the construction crew.

With this issue settled upon, we sat by the stream and BS'd about environmental issues, politics, hunting, fishing, and of course, women. While discussing the history of Siziman Bay, Vadim commented that his grandfather might well be buried near one of the gulag sites. He didn't really know what happened to him, but apparently his grandfather was taken away one night and never seen again. Later that evening after we returned to camp, Vadim gave me a couple of pieces of petrified wood from an area not too far up the beach.

Capitan Moranseff and M/V Sibirskiy 2115

The *Captain Morensef*, a small landing craft that regularly brought in our fuel and supplies, came in from Vanino in the morning. By early afternoon, the army loaded some of their equipment on board, so it looked like they were pulling out. They got their truck stuck in the river and had to have one of our log loaders help pull it out. Also today one of our young crew members was sent back to the army. I heard that he hadn't been paid in two months, so to compensate himself for this, he stole a bunch of tools. Unfortunately for him, he got caught on his way out of camp.

Cardinal left for Komsomolsk with Phillipov after breakfast but not before telling me that he intended to give Ron his termination notice before the sixteenth when he was scheduled to go out for vacation. Apparently Ron, as usual, had flown off the handle again during their standard morning meeting today. Phillipov and Chekinkov subsequently told Cardinal that they could work with me but not with Ron, so now Cardinal wanted me to take over.

Earlier, while down at the jetty, Joe and I saw a lot of fish jumping near shore, so we decided to try our luck before lunch. We had a number of strikes, and after about an hour of frustration, Joe finally caught one. Turned out the fish were pellingas, a carp-like bottom sucker fish with no teeth. Interestingly, I was told that these fish go "blind" in the winter and bury themselves in the mud. Some of them looked to be six to eight pounds. Joe brought the fish back up to the Gulag and fried it up for a snack. A white-fleshed fish with a pleasant delicate flavor, we confirmed that we would have to continue our attempts in snagging these morsels.

The next morning Joe hollered, "Yahoo," and I wondered what the hell he was so excited about. I heard him run to his room, then shortly after, come into the Gulag kitchen with a big smile, a bottle of vodka, and two shot glasses. "What's up, you old fart?" I asked. Joe replied, "After five months of being in this bloody place, I just made my first solid turd!" He smiled proudly then asked, "Do you want to see it?" I have to admit that since I hadn't been solid since arriving in Russia, I was jealous, but I replied, "You're disgusting and out of your fucking mind!" Joe set the two shot glasses down on the table and was about to open the vodka, when I reminded him it was only 8:30 in the morning. Grumbling his disappointment, Joe took the vodka back to his room, then returned to have coffee with me before we headed down to the office and log yard.

Later that morning, Joe came to my office to give me a report on what was happening in the yard. I had heard him coming down the hallway and quickly poured two glasses of cognac and handed one to him as he stepped through the door. "What's this?" he asked. I clinked my glass to his and toasted, "To your turd!" "You pot licker," he said, "a couple of hours ago you said it was too early to drink." My response was, "You're right, but I was sitting here thinking that it's five o'clock somewhere, so here's to you." We both laughed and shot the drink down, and then had another just for the hell of it.

For the next two weeks I discussed, argued, and negotiated with Sharkoff, now the Commercial Director for Dalny-Les, and the other Russian managers on Takahara's request for production of 8.1 meter sawlogs. Early on in the discussions, I learned that their primary concern was centered on the volume of overall production and the way logs are measured under the official Russian GOST Rules. Sharkoff would scribble out charts and diagrams during our discussions to make his points. His primary argument was that the small end "scaling" diameter of an 8.1 meter log would be less than that of a 7.6 meter log cut from the same tree. Subsequently, the same number of 8.1 meter logs would have less volume than that of 7.6 meter logs. He informed me that, since the crews got paid based on the volume produced during their shift, cutting longer logs would result in less pay. The operation would therefore have to cut more trees to meet production requirements demanded by the Komsomolsk office. It became clear to me that this was also apparently the reason there was a tendency to cut more 3.8 meter logs than necessary. Profitability did not seem to factor into their equation.

Since Sharkoff was a fairly analytical person, I knew that to convince him I would have to come up with my own charts and diagrams for him to review. I started by obtaining copies of the GOST volume charts from the scalers for 3.8 meter, 4.0 meter, 7.6 meter, and 8.1 meter log lengths. I then went to the log yard and measured the scaling diameters of a hundred 7.6 meter sawlogs, as well as obtaining the diameters at 3.8 meters. Back at the office, I prepared a table listing this information and projecting the average log taper, estimated the diameter at 8.1 meters. Using this data, I was able to show Sharkoff that in the Siziman Bay area, the volume difference from producing 8.1 meters versus 7.6 meters was minimal. In addition to this, I informed him that Takahara had told me we should be able to obtain a price premium of at least ten dollars per cubic meter over that paid for 7.6 meter sawlogs.

Having finally convinced him, Sharkoff took a copy of my charts, tables, and diagrams with him to help in his discussions back in Komsomolsk. I didn't know if production of 8.1 meter sawlogs was going to happen, until about a week later when the first truckload came into the log yard. I was unaware at the time, but part of the reason for the delayed production was due to having to wait for the next crew change. The current crew was under "strict" instructions from the Komsomolsk office to produce a certain volume of 7.6 meter sawlogs and as such, could not alter plans. Takahara had requested, and I negotiated for a test shipment volume of 300 cubic meters. I assumed that this was what would subsequently be produced.

There was not a wisp of wind on the morning of the eleventh, and the bay was flat calm. With the clouds hanging low against the hills, I was reminded of Southeast Alaska, which then got me thinking of fishing. Unfortunately, as I walked down the beach, I found that the damn Russians had a couple of gill nets strung out from shore which were loaded with fish. The only thing I caught was their net, costing me a lure in the process.

October 15th brought the arrival of the mid-month crew shift change. Misha, who had become my main interpreter, was heading out for his fifteen days off back home in Komsomolsk. While standing around waiting to load up the crew bus, he joked that since he had been in camp for three weeks, he was afraid his girlfriend may have forgotten him. "I feel a little different about leaving this time," he told me. "Why?" I asked. "Well," he continued, "I want to go home, but I also kind of want to stay with you guys here at Siziman." "Misha," I said as I chuckled and slapped him on the shoulder, "what you're feeling is what we Americans call insanity. Now get your butt on the bus, and we'll see you next month."

Chuck and Hubert spent most of the day messing with the satellite TV system and almost got it working. They were able to get a fix on some Russian stations but hadn't been able to locate any US satellites yet. At least we had the VCR hooked up so we could finally watch some movies.

Our fourth vessel was due in the next day, and Potarov agreed with me to load the shipment out round the clock and in an unprecedented two days. Considering the variable weather conditions and the storms this time of year, I didn't want to have the ship leave partially loaded.

Sharkoff arrived in camp around 6:00 a.m. the next morning, and not too long after that began our first confrontation. I wandered down to the office about 7:00 a.m. and asked Lena for the loading orders. To my surprise, the 300 cubic meters of 8.1 meter sawlogs was not included. I walked down the hallway to Potarov's office and asked Sharkoff about this. He abruptly said, "I do not like the price quoted, so we're not going to load these logs," and walked away. I followed behind him, explaining, "You previously agreed to the October prices, and the customer is expecting this trial shipment volume. We need to send these logs on this vessel!" I also informed him that "the customer will not pay the higher price we negotiated for the 7.6 meter sawlogs if the 8.1's are not included."

I once again showed him the volume comparisons, pricing scenarios, etc. that I had developed. Since my documentation was prepared in advance and he had nothing to counter with, he again essentially agreed with the concept. However, Sharkoff's simple reply was still, "We will not be loading the 8.1 meter logs on this vessel." He walked out the door and left me standing in the hallway wondering what the hell was going on. I went to my office, sat down at my desk, and started to fume! I grabbed Genady and went out to look for Sharkoff. I found him out in the log yard giving instructions to the crew, and I started discussing the issue with him again.

By this time it was 10:30 a.m. and the M/V *Sibirskiy 2111* was coming into berth. We argued some more, and he reluctantly agreed with me, saying that he would "instruct the crew to load the 8.1 meter logs on the vessel last" then abruptly headed off to the jetty. However, I knew that if he didn't put these logs on first, they would never get loaded. I ran up to the shop, hopped into the nearest pickup, and sped down to the jetty, getting even angrier as I went. The vessel was being tied up, and Sharkoff was waiting for the gangplank to be lowered so he could go on board and meet with the captain. I walked up to him and standing toe-to-toe, face-to-face began arguing with him again, the both of us shouting at the top of our lungs. Sharkoff finally admitted to me that he had not received authorization from the Komsomolsk office and needed to wait until after their 2:00 p.m. radio call to determine if we could load the 8.1's.

"I don't give a damn about the Komsomolsk office; this is our issue," I replied. I then turned to Genady and told him to translate what I was going to say, exactly as I said it. I turned back to Dmitry and continued, "I do not know the reason for the customer's request, but I intend to load this vessel in the order of their specification, and that means that the 8.1 meter sawlogs are to be loaded first. So, you have two choices. You will either direct the crew to load the 8.1 meter logs first, or I will throw *you* into the hold first and then load the fucking logs on top of you!"

He quietly replied, "Okay," turned, and instructed Anatoly, the crew supervisor, to load the 8.1's first. Then he calmly climbed on board the vessel to meet with the captain. I was stunned. I looked at Genady and asked him, "What the hell just happened here?" He replied, "You won." "What do you mean I won?" I asked. Genady said, "He was testing to see how far he could push you, and if you would back down. You didn't back down, you out-shouted him, and so you won!"

So concluded another lesson learned in how to deal with the Russians. Looking back at the event, I find it somewhat comical. There Sharkoff and I were, angrily shouting at the top of our lungs, pausing only as necessary to allow Genady to translate what we were saying. Throughout the entire confrontation he did so in his usual calm, mild-mannered tone of voice.

Before I left the jetty, the radio engineer, a friend of Captain Vladimir of the *Sibirskiy 2117* whom I met during that vessel's previous trip, came ashore with a gift from Vladimir and a request. "You had told Vladimir that you missed having an occasional beer here at Siziman," he said, "so he asked me to give you this." I was pleasantly surprised when he handed me a case of Sapparo Beer from Japan. "Please tell Vladimir it was kind of him to think of me and express to him my big thanks." I then asked, "What is his request?" Handing me an envelope, he said, "Vladimir asks if you could deliver this letter and $500 to his girlfriend living in Anchorage when you next return to America. She is a student at the University of Alaska." "*Neyht problem*," I said. "Tell Vladimir that I will be happy to do this for him." It was the least I could do for a case of good beer, and I figured that I could get some help from my ex-secretary there to track down Vladimir's girlfriend.

There wasn't a Russian manager in sight the entire next day, including Potarov. I didn't know why, but for the second day in a row he was stone dead drunk and in his room sleeping it off. However, Sharkoff did show up at the ship about 9:00 p.m. and changed the loading sequence that I had instructed the crew. I believe he did this intentionally just to make a point. Rather than throw him off the vessel into the bay, which is what I wanted to do, I was too tired to argue anymore with him. So, midpoint in our confrontations, I threw up my hands in disgust, turned away, and told Genady, "The hell with it. Let's go back to the Gulag and have us a beer."

About an hour later, a bloodshot-eyed Potarov walked into the Gulag kitchen lounge. Knowing that I was extremely irritated about Sharkoff's actions, he came up to talk with me about it. After his meeting with me, Potarov returned to his room and drank some more. I didn't see him again until the next day. It was then that I found out through Genady that although it would have shown weakness for him to say it to me directly, Sharkoff had apologized. "He will not interfere again with the ship loading process that you and Joe have developed." More than likely his apology was because he fouled up the procedure and realized he caused delays in the loading of the vessel. However, there also seemed to be some sort of power play going on in Komsomolsk between Cardinal, Phillipov, and Nazarkin that involved me. I was not up on what was going on, but the Russians in camp seemed to be, and their attitude toward my authority appeared to be changing.

Loading of the vessel was completed by 8:00 p.m. on the eighteenth, and it left Siziman Bay just before midnight with 4,000 cubic meters of sawlogs on board. Our crew had now broken two previous Russian ship loading standards. They had consistently loaded more volume of logs on the Sibirskiy-class vessel than ever done before. In addition, they had twice now completed loading in less than four days, in fact doing so with this vessel in an unprecedented 48½ hours.

Early the next morning, I telephoned Cardinal in Komsomolsk to discuss a fax I had received from the Philadelphia office. "John," I said, "what's with this letter addressed to Sergei Phillipov designating me as general manager in Ron's absence?" To my surprise, the letter also placed emphasis on increasing my role in the marketing of Siziman Bay's production. I continued, "I guess Bailey wants me to be involved in some meeting in Khabarovsk coming up on Monday between Shasta Corp. and Dalny-Les."

Cardinal angrily shouted, "I don't care what Bailey wants, now you just listen to me!" Still irritated from him not returning my calls the morning of the ship loading incident with Sharkoff, I cut him short. "Don't you dare talk to me in that manner. If you want to get our business relationship off to a good start, you'd better treat me with some respect!" All the while I was thinking to myself, *What an asshole.* Cardinal knew that I had a direct line to the top folks in Philadelphia, and he didn't like it at all. Calming down a little, he then informed me that "Sergei will contact you tomorrow and invite you to the meeting in Khabarovsk." I wanted to say that this didn't mean diddly-squat to me, but instead said, "Sounds good." "I'll call you from Khabarovsk," he added, "to discuss other issues before you leave camp." After saying good-bye, I hung up the telephone, turned to Joe, and said, "What a dumb ass!"

October 19th was Vladislav Shukalov's birthday. To celebrate, we expats invited him up to the Gulag that evening for a few drinks. Vladislav, one of the Russian foremen, was genuinely well liked by all the expats. His jovial personality and quick humor had helped to ease tensions on many occasions. He was seldom seen without a newsboy style cap covering his reddish-blonde hair, and usually wore a suit jacket regardless of whether he was wearing slacks or blue-jeans. A neatly trimmed moustache stretched out like a fuzzy caterpillar above his almost continuous smile. Even when criticized or reprimanded by his supervisors, he would jokingly comment that he was *papaya'd again.* Vladislav had never seen a papaya before, and he got a big kick out of it when Joe jokingly gave him a couple of the fruits as a present. To make this occasion "international," we had Russian vodka and Canadian whiskey along with the usual sausages, bread, and salads. Boris Nesterov and Tanya played their guitar and keyboard while leading the singing of Russian folk songs. Previously a teacher in Komsomolsk, Boris was one of our more proficient translators. A soft spoken, even-tempered, middle-aged gentleman, he was also a devoted Christian. Unfortunately, like many fathers with a young daughter, Boris was experiencing the typical issues associated with raising a teenager. I could see that this troubled him and made it difficult at times to be away from his family for such long periods of time. Tanya was the camp cleaning supervisor and also in charge of the laundry room. What we would call a large-boned woman, Tanya stood about six feet two inches in height. Although not an attractive woman physically, Tanya had such a sweetheart of a personality and was always willing to help in any way that she could. Boris had overheard me singing John Denver's "Whiskey Basin Blues" the previous day and insisted that I sing it for the group. During the festivities, I was once again amazed that despite their current hardships, the Russian people were, for the most part, always in good spirits.

When he telephoned the next day, Cardinal was a little more civil to me. "I intend for you to be the number two man in Russia," he said, but didn't really tell me what that meant. "I want you to work closely with Phillipov." Then before hanging up, he added that I would find out more when I got to Khabarovsk.

I left camp the next day to catch the early morning train from Visakogorny to Khabarvosk. I had not expected to make this trip but was happy to get a break from camp. The road trip to Visakogorny was interesting as always. Although relatively uneventful, we did encounter the usual deep mud holes and large boulders that violently rocked the truck, making it impossible to sleep. And, of course, the river crossing on a collapsed bridge added to the "adventure" of the trip. I met Potarov on the road, coming back from a one-day trip home. He was drunk again, and I thought it funny that I hadn't even noticed that he had been gone.

Train Station in Visakogorny

I arrived in Visakogorny four hours prior to the train, and with nothing else to do, I sat around the station just trying to stay warm. The train station, although obviously having seen its better days, was still one of the more attractive buildings in the village. Built in the mid-1940s by Japanese prisoners of war, the two-story building was made entirely of wood. What appeared to be a small belfry sat atop the roof, the bell long since removed. Painted olive green with decoratively carved forest-green trim, the building was a striking difference from the standard cement slab structures of the post-war communist era. The lobby area inside was dimly lit with only two bench seats and lacked an efficient heating system. Other than myself, the station remained empty and eerily quiet the entire time. The train finally arrived at 1:55 a.m. and quickly departed five minutes later.

I slept all the way to Komsomolsk, waking up only when the attendant knocked on the door announcing our impending arrival at 9:30 a.m. Once the train departed again an hour later, I found out quickly that the compartment next to mine was occupied by two young mothers. One of the children, a girl approximately one year old and just learning to walk, was a little cutie. She kept coming into my compartment, smiling, laughing, and wanting to play. So play we did, at one time keeping me occupied for over two hours. I was reminded of the earlier days spent playing with my daughter when she was that age. God, how I missed her.

When the train arrived in Khabarovsk that evening, I was met by a driver for Dalny-Les and taken to the Parus Hotel. Unfortunately, I had to have dinner with Cardinal. After talking with him for a while, I needed a drink and went to the bar for a nightcap. I met a couple of young kids in their early twenties and ended up talking with them until closing time. The younger Russians loved to practice their English whenever they could. I always enjoyed sitting with them, finding it fun to learn and talk about our different lifestyles.

The next day I met with another one of Joe's friends, Vladimir Golubov, who took me to his office and then up to his apartment for lunch and to meet his family. Emma, his mother-in-law, was a professor at the university. His wife, Tatyana, was an attorney. Tonya, a beautiful twenty-five-year-old brunette, worked with Vladimir in his office, and his thirteen-year-old daughter, Sveta, was in school specializing in English. Tatiana was an extremely attractive petite woman, which helped to explain why they had a five-month-old son. However, it was Tonya that caught my attention after following her up the stairway, noticing her shapely body, long legs, and tight-fitting short skirt. Unfortunately, it was Sveta who was learning English and not Tonya, so communication with her—at least how I would have preferred it to be—was impossible.

After lunch, Vladimir and Tatyana took me to the local public market which was a bustling, chaotic, but fascinating place. The large, open building contained row after row of countertops filled with vegetables, meat, fish, and cut flowers. All the clerks (primarily women) wore white hats and thigh-length white coats similar to those worn by nurses. One corner seemed to be solely Chinese food products and another was Korean. The area outside the building consisted of small shops, booths, tents, and tables loaded with various items. Clothes, bakery items, cigarettes, cassette tapes, videos, magazines, fishing gear, automobile and household spare parts, and just about anything else you could think of were available for purchase. A grouping of tents in one area seemed to be primarily Chinese selling various products brought in from that country, mostly the cheap junk like you'd find in one of those dollar stores back in the States.

Leaving the marketplace, we walked up to Lenin Square and then through the city center along Muravyev-Amursky Street. Since it was Sunday, many of the shops were closed, so we continued our walk down to the park along the Amur River. Numerous street vendors were parked along the way, selling food items such as *sasiska*, a hot dog wrapped in baked bread. Small kiosks sold magazines, soda, and warm beer. Sergei was a highly educated individual with exceptional skills in the English language. He told me that previously he was relatively high in the local area's Communist Party, but now proudly exclaimed that he was "a capitalist." As we walked along, he commented that he "truly understands that the communist way was wrong and not the best for Russia."

Chuck and Hubert had arrived to Khabarovsk on the morning train. It was October 24th and they were catching the afternoon flight back to the States for their trip "out." Having time to kill, they stopped by the hotel to have breakfast and say good-bye. Hubert would be coming back to Siziman Bay in December. Chuck's wife was due to have their baby in a couple of months, so if he came back, it would not be until March at the earliest. I would miss him. He was a good mechanic, a fun person to have around and the Russians really liked him a lot. I don't know how these guys did it though, staying away from their family for two months at a time. If my ex-wife had not said to get the hell out of her life, I don't think I could do it. When they left, I smiled, thinking about why the Russians had always chuckled when Chuck referred to Hubert as Huey. Curious about this, one day I asked Misha about it. "It is because Huey sounds a lot like *hooey*," he replied, "which is a dirty reference to penis, like the American slang 'cock.'" I never did have the heart to inform Hubert of this and certainly didn't let anyone else in on this either.

I was scheduled to fly back to Siziman Bay later in the morning in a MI-8 helicopter that Dalny-Les had chartered. At the airport, the six of us piled into the helicopter, sitting on the two benches located along the walls. My attention quickly focused on the fifty-five-gallon fuel tank opposite from where I was seated. As we began our take-off, I commented to Cardinal that something didn't feel quite right and that the helicopter seemed to be riding rougher than usual. He laughed it off, but after about five minutes into the flight, red lights flashed on the instrument panel.

The pilot quickly turned the helicopter around, headed back to the airport, and abruptly dropped to the runway. We had barely touched the ground when he shut the engines down as the copilot opened the door and urged us to leave quickly. We were met by a fire truck which fortunately did not have to be used. I never learned what the problem actually was, but after an hour of standing around on the tarmac, we got into another helicopter and headed off to Komsomolsk to pick up Nazarkin. Shortly after leaving Komsomolsk, we stopped at the village of Selikino, located along the Amur River, to fuel up before continuing on to Siziman Bay.

Once we arrived safely at camp, the three OPIC representatives were shown to their rooms up in the Gulag before being given the grand tour of the camp, sort yard, and dock facilities. Dinner that evening contained, in the standard Russian tradition, an ample supply of vodka and wine. A few minutes after Cardinal and Phillipov had made their obligatory toasts of welcoming visitors to Russia and in particular to Siziman Bay, I stood up and raised my shot glass. "I'd like to make a toast," I announced, "to the friendships and cooperation that continues to grow here at Siziman Bay. While here at camp, we are not Amerikanskis, we are not Russkis, but we are Sizimanskis, and that is what will make this operation successful. So, to Sizimanskis!" at which time everyone stood (with the exception of Nazarkin), raised their glass, and shot down their vodka. I found it interesting that Nazarkin was not drinking at all on this trip and figured that someone back in the States must have come down real hard on him for his actions during his last visit to camp. It might also explain the cold grimacing stare that he would occasionally shoot my way. Lord how I despised that man.

The next morning, Joe looked like death warmed over. I felt a little sorry for the old fart. He was up all night sick as a dog, puking his guts out, having partied with the Russians until after midnight. I've learned quickly that Russian vodka is a killer drink, especially since the way they drink it is in straight "choot choot" shots. The trouble is that after six or seven choot choots, look out! Joe ended up sleeping most of the day, and by late afternoon still felt like something you scrape off the bottom of your shoe. Cardinal was quite hung over this morning as well but managed to make it through the OPIC tour of the woods operations.

The group left camp on the helicopter shortly after noon, and life began to return to normal. Potarov tried to get Joe to have one shot of vodka to "fix him right up," calling it "the hair of the dog that bit you," but all Joe could think about was vomiting. I could tell that Potarov was feeling a huge relief having the big bosses from Komsomolsk gone. I think he just needed someone to relax and talk with, so I ended up sharing half a bottle with him. This really was the last thing that I needed to do, drink vodka at 2:30 in the afternoon, but he felt better, and we ended up having a good heart-to-heart discussion.

In the evening, two Russians apparently got into a fight over a bottle of vodka, and one guy hit the other across the head with a metal pipe. He cracked the guy's skull wide open, and Doc ended up driving him to the hospital in Visakogorny. Before leaving, Doc told me the guy was in critical condition and might not make it into town. Not much was being said about the incident, but I was told there was to be a criminal investigation undertaken. Doc was a real nice guy, always pleasant and in a good mood. I thought it kind of sad though that before perestroika, he was an important surgeon at one of the hospitals in Komsomolsk but now was reduced to what essentially was a First Aid Technician babysitting a bunch of drunken Russians.

Sam Colson, one of the Americans working out of the Komsomolsk office, was sitting in the kitchen lounge when I got there in the morning. As I poured my first cup of coffee for the day, he immediately started to complain about the Gulag, the camp, Pritchard, the Philadelphia office, everything. Not in the mood for it, I shouted, "Damn it Sam, ever since I came to Russia I have told everyone that I don't really care about how it was or what happened in the past. I'm not going to listen to finger-pointing and accusations, and I don't what to hear this crap from you!" I sat down, and irritated with me, Sam left. Later in the day, while he apparently was complaining about me down at the shop, Newton shut him down. "Sam, what Paul said is right on, and you basically have two choices. You can either work with him or not, and if you're not, then you might as well pack up and head back to Komsomolsk." Sam apparently got the message since from that day on, if he did do any complaining, he kept it to himself.

Potarov tracked me down in the sort yard that afternoon, all excited that he was going back to Visakogorny, and his wife, for a week. It had been quite a while since he had been out of camp, and from his comments over the past couple of weeks, I think his marriage was in trouble. He was all smiles as he said good-bye and climbed into the UAZ "*Roosski* Jeep." He invited me to join him and his wife in town sometime in the near future, and said, "*Dahsveedahneeyah*," and sped off down the road. I hadn't seen him that happy in a long time—at least not while sober.

Chekinkov was really starting to work with Joe and me on log sort quality and attempting to maximize value through proper manufacturing of sawlogs rather than focusing only on production volume. The three of us spent most of the day out in the woods working with operators on this issue, then going over it again during the 8:00 p.m. meeting with the supervisors. Another fight broke out in the evening, apparently over vodka again. I can hardly believe some of these idiot crew members we get here, but at least no one was seriously hurt this time.

Chekinkov was preparing to leave camp, but before going, he came by my office to say good-bye. With his arm around my shoulder, he informed me that "while Potarov and I are not in camp, you should make the decisions. I trust you." His open expression of confidence in me really caught me off guard. The general mood of cooperation and communication between the Russians and Americans had significantly improved since Pritchard left. After Chekinkov left, Joe commented that "this operation is actually beginning to become fun and exciting. You know," he continued, "I had decided that on my next out I was either going to stay in Alaska or go to Lake Baikal and work for another outfit. But I think now I'll seriously consider coming back to this loony outfit."

"You'd better come back, you old fart," I replied. "I need your help keeping my sanity around this place." "I didn't know how much you cared," he said and chuckled as he placed his hand on my shoulder. Jabbing him in the ribs with my elbow, I answered, "Shit, get out of here and go down to the log yard where you belong." "Come on, Misha," he said while leaving. "Let's go see the girls down at the scale shack where we're really appreciated." I just shook my head and thought to myself that I was really going to miss Joe while he was out. I was glad that he was changing his mind about staying on with us. Newton, scheduled to leave for the States in a couple of weeks, was also favorably reconsidering coming back in February after taking care of business back home.

The evening of November 1ˢᵗ brought us our first snowstorm. Satellite reception for the television went haywire as a result, and being tired of messing around with the dish, we decided to watch the *Dances with Wolves* video instead. Karl Jansen, a Canadian from Montreal, Quebec, was mildly disappointed since he had been following the vote on Quebec separating from the rest of Canada. He had never commented on his preference regarding this issue, but eventually we learned it was voted down by 53 percent to 47 percent. Karl seemed like a nice guy, but was very quiet and tended to keep to himself. I heard from numerous individuals that the Russians did not like him; in fact, the previous day a couple of the Russian mechanics told him to go to hell. Other than perhaps maybe Pritchard, the Russians have never said anything like this to any of us other expats. Kind of funny though, the people back in Philadelphia thought the Russians loved him!

The day of crew change always brought unexpected events, and the November shifting was no exception. Potarov came into the office in the early morning on the second and asked me to come with him to his room. When I got there, he introduced me to his wife, Natasha, who had apparently come back to camp late last night with him on one of the crew buses. With his arm around her waist, Potarov proudly said, "Paul, you need a good Russian wife like I have." Potarov offered me some chai (tea) and we sat down to chat for awhile. The conversation turned to the differences in food in the United States versus in Russia. Natasha asked, *What is your favorite food that you have had here in Russia?* I replied "Borscht, of course!" Nikolay exclaimed, *Natasha makes a delicious borscht. See, now if you had a good Russian wife like I have, you could have borscht more often.* Noticing that Natasha had a sore throat, I quickly changed the subject by offering to give her some of my cold medicine I had brought with me from the States.

Misha, had also come back and had brought Sergei Phillipov's son, Zhenya (Jack), in with him. Zhenya was apparently learning English, and Phillipov sent him to Siziman Bay to get some exposure to the language from us Americans in camp. Ivan Karilikoff was also back in camp, and it didn't take more than an hour for him to stir up our first confrontation of his shift. Poor guy, he would never win, and I really hated tromping on him like I had to, but the man just refused to work any other way. Mikhail, one of my favorite 980 operators, was back in the sort yard. When I went to see him, he kept turning his head away, not wanting to look directly at me while I was talking with him. When he finally did face me, I blurted out, "What the hell happened to you?" He had a huge black eye, apparently caused by his wife when she cold cocked him during a fight the night before returning to camp. Mikhail was such a lovable, easygoing guy. He looked a little like Phil Collins and worked like a son-of-a-gun for Joe and me. I just couldn't imagine what he did to get smacked like that.

Later that evening, I was sitting in the Gulag kitchen when suddenly a loud bloodcurdling scream came from within the bathroom area. Joe soon burst into the kitchen shouting, "Those bloody Russian heathens. One of them took a shit in the shower stall, and I almost stepped in it! What's worse, the bastard sat there long enough to smoke two cigarettes!" Laughing hysterically, I followed Joe into the shower area to check it out, and sure enough, there it was right on top of the drain. "You're right, Joe," I said, "he apparently wasn't in any big hurry." With a quick slap to the back of my head, Joe grumbled, "You pot licker," then started to laugh with me.

In the past, we've had guys try to stand on the toilet seat while doing their deed, but this was an unusual first. I hollered for Genady and told him to find Potarov and inform him about this. "Ask him to get someone to come up to thoroughly clean this shower stall out for us." When he heard of this incident, Potarov immediately came up to the Gulag to apologize to us expats. He explained that many of the workers at Siziman come from small villages along the railway and have homes with no toilets. "They are used to just pulling down their pants and squatting over a hole." Obviously holding back his laughter, but with a big grin he added that "the shower drain must have looked normal to whoever did this." "Well," I said, "considering how cold it is outside and the two cigarettes that were left, whoever it was must have thought the warm stall was pretty classy." Potarov was really embarrassed by the incident though, and from that point on, the Gulag was off-limits to Russian crew members, unless invited there by one of the Americans.

The one individual that I was real tired of seeing barge into the Gulag kitchen uninvited, without knocking, and at any time of the day or night, was Ivan Karlikoff. On the evening of the third when he rushed in and interrupted our relaxation, I tried to reason with him, but to no satisfaction. I finally said, "Look Ivan, we Americans are over here for two to three months at a time, and the Gulag is our home away from home. I would not come into your home uninvited, and I suspect that you do not go into other Russians' rooms in camp uninvited. As such, I must ask that you respect our privacy." His quick response was, "I do not like that Americans are here in Russia, and—" Cutting him short, I jumped up and angrily shouted, "I don't care about that, we are here in Siziman Bay whether you like it or not." Karlikoff was a staunch believer in communism and generally was not happy with perestroika. "Since you have such a strong dislike for us," I continued, "then it's all the more reason to give us some space." Ivan was not liked by most of the Russians here in camp, and I did feel somewhat sorry for him about this, but with his attitude, the little shit brought it on by himself.

I believe the doctor in camp for this shift was a little light on his feet, so to speak. After the other expats had gone to sleep and while I was washing up some dishes, he appeared at the door. I said, "Hi Doc," as he shook my hand. He immediately put his arm around my waist, which I assumed was a gesture of friendship. As he was about to put his head on my shoulder, I thought, *What the hell*, and shouted out, "*Neeeyht*," abruptly pulling away from him. Using certain sign language familiar in most countries, along with some choice words, I made it clear to him that I was about to punch his lights out and he'd better back off. He left, and I thought to myself that this was kind of like the "icing on the cake" of an otherwise really strange day at Siziman Bay. In the morning I mentioned this to Potarov and this particular doctor was sent home on the next crew bus back to town and never seen again.

The next evening, I had just returned to the Gulag after a few hours of eating, drinking, and dancing down at one of the scaler's room when Joe rushed into the kitchen. "Come on buddy, we're going down to the jetty for a swim." "Joe," I responded, "it's late and colder than a witch's tit in December outside. I've got a good buzz going, so the last thing I want to do is jump into the bay and freeze my ass off." Not able to convince me to go, Joe grabbed a towel from his room, hopped into the pickup, and drove off into the darkness. He returned about an hour later, wide-eyed, looking like a drowned rat and needing some coffee to help warm him up.

"So, how was it you crazy old fart?" I asked. With a big smile on his face, Joe replied, "My pecker shrank to the size of a baby's as soon as I hit the water. Ohhhh, but to see Natasha's big tits exposed through her wet bra and those white panties showing off that bushy black beaver of hers was well worth it!" "I've said it before Joe, you're a dirty old man and out of your fucking mind, but I guess that's why I love ya! You're lucky you didn't drown." Joe popped me one on the top of my head and said, "You pot licker, I'm sober, cold, and need a drink. Got anything?" I went to my room, brought back a bottle of cognac, and then downed a couple more shots with him before heading off to bed. From that night on, and in part to keep this Natasha identified from the other three Natashas, she was forever nicknamed "Big Beav."

The Russian banya (sauna) is not only a facility that an individual uses for their daily—or more likely their weekly—cleansing, but it is often more a social setting where friends, coworkers, and business associates meet to bond. Siziman Bay's banya was in a rustic-looking log cabin of which two-thirds was the banya area and the remainder served as the laundry room. The actual banya portion of the building was of the typical design consisting of three rooms. First, the entry room served to separate the often freezing elements on the outside from the warmth inside. It also was the place where you would hang your "outer" clothes and store your boots. The next room was the changing room, but also served as an area to eat, drink, and relax. One side of the room was lined with benches, clothes hooks, and a continuous shelf. The other side had a small "trench" in the floor with a wooden walkway covering it. This is where you would fill a bucket with as cold of water as you could handle and pour it over your body after being in the sauna. A proper Russian-style banya is one in which the heat is generated by a wood fire with the hot air then circulated through a brick "fireplace" with rocks in it. Steam is created by taking a ladle of water from a bucket and throwing it on the hot rocks.

I really do not particularly care for the actual sauna portion of the banya experience, but as I was now General Manager of the operation and representative for the US partners, I often could not refuse to go. One such instance involved a day spent with representatives of the local forestry department. The head honcho of this group had taken a keen interest in my Yamaha snowmobile and had been asking my Russian counterparts to "donate" it to his agency. When asked numerous times about this during the day, my answer was always, "Absolutely not, no fucking way." Later that evening, after dinner and considerable choot-choots of vodka, I was treated to the Russian birch branch experience by this guy in the banya.

Usually this is an extremely invigorating treatment whereby the birch branch, complete with its green leaves, is dipped into a bucket of water then methodically slapped over your body, increasing the intensity of the heat. However with this guy, I thought I was going to lose all the layers of my skin and was surprised that I did not emerge with blood dripping down my back. I believe he was really ticked off about the snowmobile and the fact that he would not be leaving with it in the morning. However, with another toast and a shot of vodka we were good buddies once more.

Expats' Gulag Kitchen

Misha found me having coffee in the Gulag's kitchen lounge early the next day and told me that Potarov had asked for a meeting with me in his office. When I arrived, Karlikoff was already there complaining about me. "Nikolay, *dohbra ohtra, khak de la*" (good morning, how are you?), I greeted as I walked through the door. "Paul, you are wrong, and it was stupid of you to schedule a ship for Monday," Karlikoff immediately shouted at me. "Your inventory data is incorrect, and there is not enough pulpwood to load the vessel!" "Ivan," I replied, "I have no doubt that we have enough volume of pulp logs in the log yard for this vessel. However, if I am wrong I will take full responsibility since I was the one who requested the ship." "You are stupid," Karlikoff immediately responded. I was getting increasingly tired of this little shit always calling me stupid. However, I calmly replied, "Ivan, if I am wrong I will apologize to you. But if I am right, and you attempt to interfere with the ship-loading operations, I will personally load you onto the ship as a non-standard length log and send you to Japan!" Potarov burst out laughing at this, and Karlikoff angrily stomped out of the room. It was amazing how much turmoil that Karlikoff had created since returning to camp—to be expected, but amazing just the same.

As I left the office to go back up to the Gulag, it suddenly hit me that I was seeing only two of the six or seven dogs normally around camp. While stopping off in the cookhouse to grab a pastry for a snack, I casually asked the cook about this. In English he simply said, "Ate." I chuckled at his response, but it was clear that he was not joking. I had to admit, though, that dinner on occasion during the last couple of weeks did have some unidentifiable meat to it. Tossing off the thought, I just shook my head as I turned and walked back outside.

Lunch sucked again today. I took a bowl of soup, which as usual was good, then went up to the Gulag and opened up a can of Spam. Potarov came into my office later in the day and presented me with a Russian wool coat with matching wool pants. Although heavy due to the incredibly tightly woven fabric, the outfit was extremely warm. Misha commented that I would appreciate these later this winter. After he left, I thought about how much had changed since my coming to Siziman Bay in August. The Russians really seemed to like me here, and I couldn't help but feeling good about this. As for myself, I generally liked them, and although we had our differences at times, this was to be expected. For the most part, we got along very well, both socially and on operations.

I think the whole can of Spam I had for lunch was too much of a shock to my system. By three in the afternoon, I felt real bad and decided to go up to my room to sleep it off. I woke up three hours later to the smell of pellingas being cooked up by Newton. None of us wanted to venture down to the kitchen and take the chance of what might be offered, so he, Joe, Colson, and I feasted on fish, canned corn, and fruit cocktail. Thank God for blind fish and sharp hooks, for without them I'd be losing more weight than I already was. Jansen, for some reason, again declined to join us. I had noticed that he usually tended to keep to himself and not participate in any free time with the rest of us.

November 5th came with a beautiful sunrise, clear blue sky, a light breeze, and cold temperatures. Ice was beginning to form close to shore near the jetty. There was a huge school of pellingas circling the shoreline, so Joe and I grabbed our fishing gear and snagged some more fish for dinner. After filleting them, I handed them over to Newton who, using a relatively simple recipe of flour, miscellaneous spices, and lemon, did his magic in the frying pan. Even Misha, who says he doesn't like fish, had a couple of pieces and asked for more. Apparently he had never had fish prepared this way.

Before getting on the radio for his morning communication to the Komsomolsk office, Potarov wanted to meet with me and discuss log shipment alternatives for the remainder of the season. Sharkoff had given him an "order" to have a shipment of sawlogs during the week of the twentieth, another one the week of the twenty-seventh, and two more shipments, including one of pulpwood, during the first two weeks of December. I blew him away when I informed him that "I already had a preliminary schedule for shipments on the seventeenth, twenty-second, and the thirtieth," and that I was just waiting for the signed Fixture Notices to be faxed to us. "Nikolay, tell the Komsomolsk office that you and I had already worked this schedule out." Siziman Bay's reputation had gotten out, and shipping companies were knocking on our sales rep's door to get involved in the operation. "I spoke with the folks in the Seattle office," Joe said. "They are amazed at the recent turn around in production here at Siziman." "Yah," I replied, "big difference from what was happening back in August when I first got here." Joe continued, "They also said we received another good report from the Japanese on our last shipment, especially the quality and diameter of the 8.1 meter sawlogs you sent out."

Later in the day, Misha told me that Karlikoff got into an argument with Potarov over the proposed shipment schedule. Apparently

Potarov literally picked Karlikoff up by the collar and kicked him out of his office. By "kick" I mean just that—like how you would kick a football.

Early evening, Phillipov's son Jack, who had been gone fishing out on the Chichimara River the past few days, stopped by the Gulag and gave me eight grayling. These were greatly appreciated and saved us expats, with the exception of Karl Jansen, again from having to have dinner down at the kitchen. Karl just didn't seem to be working out, and pretty much just stayed to himself. Potarov, for one, was not happy that he had come back.

I woke up at 5:00 a.m. to a blizzard. Before ending by midday, there was over three inches accumulated on the ground. You would think that he would stop asking for trouble, but this morning Karlikoff got into another argument with Potarov and told him he was fired! It seems that Karlikoff had forgotten that he worked for Potarov, not the other way around. Potarov later joked with me that he was beginning to like my idea of shipping Karlikoff off to Japan. He also surprised me by telling me he "appreciated what we've done together to get the production up, load ships efficiently, and working without confrontations."

I had just returned from the jetty and mentioned to him that there was no ship in sight. Potarov then informed me that a significant storm was approaching our area. Throughout the day, I was becoming more nervous as we waited for the ship to arrive and finally heard that it hadn't even left Vanino until 4:00 p.m. This meant there was nothing we could do until its arrival to Siziman Bay sometime shortly before daybreak the next day. Since November 7th is a Russian holiday in celebration of the 1917 Revolution, not much work was going to occur anyway.

Potarov finally fired Karlikoff and put him on the evening crew bus back to Visakogorny, so with any luck we wouldn't see him around anymore. One pain-in-the-ass taken care of, but with Sharkoff coming into camp the next morning, I couldn't help but wonder what conflict I'd have to deal with during ship loading this time.

The storm reached our area sooner than predicted, and by early the next day, we were hit with a cyclone—the first I had ever experienced. During the morning high tide, waves were sending an almost constant spray over the top of the jetty. The outer channel buoy had been pushed from its original location about three hundred yards out in the bay to up into the berth area of the dock. The *M/V Sibirskiy 2111* had been forced to turn back for safe port in Vanino to wait out the storm and was now expected to return on the tenth. In less than a twenty-four-hour period, temperatures went from minus 25 degrees C to 5 degrees C. Over eighteen inches of snow fell before turning to a heavy rain by late evening. Winds reached speeds in excess of one hundred miles per hour, pushing six-to-eight-foot waves up onto the beach.

Later that evening, concerned about what was happening at the jetty, Joe and I took one of the pickup trucks down to monitor the situation. Once again, waves were already crashing over the jetty as we parked the truck, and there was still two hours until the 11:30 p.m. high tide. Strong gusting winds rocked the truck, and spray from the waves covered us at regular intervals. Knowing that there was nothing we could do, we headed back to the Gulag and broke out a couple of bottles of whiskey. Along with Chuck, Hubert, and Misha, we made the best of the situation as the wind shook and heavy rain pelted the Gulag all night long. Colson was driving the rest of us nuts. He was all upset and worried because I showed him a fax of a weather map which indicated that the storm was going to last five to seven days with continued heavy snowfall. He was scheduled to fly out of Khabarovsk early next week, and I was also concerned, but it was because I wanted him out of there as quickly as possible.

The next morning, Joe and I went down to the jetty to check on how it had survived. It hadn't. The roadway leading out to the dock had been completely washed away at several points. The half-mile of road adjacent to the beach accessing the rock pit no longer existed. Many of the huge boulders used for armor rock had been washed away from the entire front portion of the jetty. The west pier of the berth area had lost much of its log decking, and the rock surfacing was now at the bottom of the bay. Most of the three decks of logs which were to be loaded on our next shipment were gone. The steel "lighthouse" had been moved about five feet back from its original position. Both marker buoys, still attached to their anchors, were now lying on the beach. With the *Sibirskiy 2111* scheduled to arrive tomorrow morning, I thought we were flat out of luck. Since there was nothing more we could do, Joe and I went back to the Gulag for coffee, leaving the Russians to deal with the repair preparations.

Two soldiers from the army outpost up the beach wandered into camp mid morning. The other soldiers had already left over a couple of months ago, and these poor guys were now without fuel, electricity, and food. One of them told me they hadn't had any outside communications since the others pulled out, and he believed they had been forgotten. They greatly appreciated that I let them use the telephone to call their wives and families, and before returning to their base, Potarov allowed them to have lunch with the crew. They were to come back the next day, and I spoke with Potarov about maybe trading food for work until they either got additional supplies or were sent home.

The storm continued throughout the day, and although winds reached as high as eighty miles per hour during the night, the overall intensity of the system had decreased. During breakfast, I was informed that the access road leading out of Siziman Bay to Visakogorny was impassable. Wind-thrown trees had fallen across roughly two-thirds of the twenty kilometers of road from camp on up to the pass. Potarov had already sent crews and equipment out to begin work on it, but he estimated it would take four to five days before clearing would be completed. Adding to the sense of urgency of this was the fact that we were down to maybe six days of food left in camp.

Working twenty-four hours a day, to my amazement the Russians repaired the road and dock facility sufficient enough and in time to bring the *Sibirskiy 2111* into berth shortly after its arrival on the morning of the tenth. This was my first lesson on never underestimating what the Russians could do when push came to shove. Another storm was approaching, so I was in a hurry to get the vessel loaded and out of there. Although the dock repair was completed by 3:00 p.m., for some reason the captain did not bring the vessel in until three hours later. To make matters worse, Potarov and Sharkoff got into a major confrontation over who was in charge of the loading operations. Potarov finally won the battle, and loading started at 8:00 p.m. I helped get the loading activities off in the right direction and went to bed at 10:00 p.m. Unfortunately, Sharkoff was being a mule's ass again, and in the middle of the night, he changed that direction and loaded some logs that I wanted to wait on shipping.

I woke up the next morning to a beautiful sunny day, but I thought this was just "the calm before the storm." There was another typhoon just seventy miles to the east of us near Sakhalin Island and coming our way. Winds were only supposed to be gusting up to fifty-five miles per hour, so I was hopeful that all would be well with the dock and vessel should the storm hit us during loading operations. The captain made it very clear to me that he was not happy to be this far north this late in the year and would not return to Siziman Bay until next spring. Fortunately, the weather remained favorable, and the vessel departed without incident a couple of days later.

Now, the situation at Siziman Bay following the typhoon was not all bad. We soon learned of what was probably the only benefit to come from the storm—fresh frozen scallops! Apparently the waves had scoured the bottom of the shallow bay, throwing hundreds of huge scallops up on shore, which then quickly froze as temperatures dropped back to below freezing following the passing of the storm. Subsequently, we cooked scallops every day and every way we could for the next week and a half.

"Mornin' you old fart," I greeted Joe as he walked into my office. "Good morning, El General," he replied. Joe jokingly added, "By the way, you look more like a bum than a General Manager." You see, my jeans were unable to withstand the extreme hot water and harsh detergent used by Tanya and her father in the laundry room, and each pair had at least one torn knee. Misha, always trying to learn English terms, asked Joe to explain what "bum" meant, which he did. I shouldn't have asked him what the Russian word for "bum" was, but I did. Misha paused for a second and replied, "*Beecht.*" "*Beecht?*" Joe exclaimed. "I like that. '*Pavel Beecht*' fits you just right."

Once he finished laughing, Joe slapped me on the back and asked, "What's up today?" "Well," I said, "first off, I heard that two Russian ships sank during the last storm. Apparently one of them hit the beach on Sakhalin Island." Joe commented, "I think we were awful damn lucky with the Sibirskiy." "You got that right," I answered. "The shipping companies are real concerned about coming up to Siziman Bay this time of year; not many good places to hide if a storm comes up quickly." "We got another ship coming in though, don't we?" he asked. "I know of a vessel sitting empty in Vladivostok, but the captain refuses to come here," I answered. "I understand that one is scheduled to arrive here on the twenty-third. But Joe, you can believe it when you see it!"

Later in the day, I was sitting in the office when the telephone rang. When I answered, an excited voice screamed, "What's this I hear about the Russians serving dog for dinner?" It was Cardinal in Philadelphia. This was news to me, and I asked where in the hell he heard this from. "One of the other expats had called and left a message complaining about being fed dog." I told John that I really doubted that this was true, and "even if it was, it was probably the best tasting meat I've had at camp since I've arrived!" However, I was able to calm him down, and told him that I would follow up on the rumor and let him know. This conversation again got me thinking about how I had noticed fewer dogs around camp over the past week or so. I left my office and went to find Misha to discuss this with him and see if he knew anything. When I told him about what I had heard, he said, "No, there is no way that they would feed dog from the kitchen." In addition, he also said that he hadn't really noticed any fewer dogs around.

The next day, Misha and I went out to inspect the logging operations. It was upon our arrival to the second harvest site I learned that while dog was not being served in the kitchen, this crew from Visakogorny was roasting them over the campfire for lunch. Knowing that I would never change their habits, I gathered the crew together and told them that under no circumstances did I want Sabakha to end up like this. She was my dog and not to be killed—and they had better make sure nothing happened to her! I was leaving for my month vacation in a few days, so when we got back to camp, I immediately went to Potarov to discuss this issue with him. He assured me that my dog would be in camp upon my return from the States and that no one would harm her.

Three days later I received a copy of a fax sent to Gordon James, our sales representative, informing him that the *M/V Sibirskiy 2117* had problems with its documentation. If the vessel was to go through the Port of Vanino for clearance, it would be arrested. Subsequently, it would not be coming to Siziman Bay as scheduled. I showed it to Joe saying, "I told you not to believe it until you saw it! By the way, have you seen Potarov? I haven't seen him all day, and I need to talk with him." Joe replied, "I heard he's been bumming vodka off everyone, so I suppose the old bear is in his room drunk or sleeping it off." "Damn," I said. "I sure wish I could find out more on what's going on between him and Komsomolsk." By afternoon, the weather took a turn for the worse; the wind had picked up and heavy snow was falling. It was only two days until I was to leave for the States, so I hoped it wouldn't last.

Good fortune was apparently with me, as the next morning I woke up to a beautiful sunny day without a cloud in the sky. I felt uneasy about leaving camp at this time with all the Russian power plays going on, but after 3½ months, I was worn out and needed to get out of there to recharge. It's funny, but I also felt strange about leaving Siziman Bay. I was looking forward to getting back to the States and seeing my kids, but I thought that I needed to seriously start thinking about where I wanted to call home. I certainly needed more than an eight-foot by fourteen-foot storage room.

Finally the day of my departure came, and I was anxious to go, having already packed my bag the previous night. People had been coming up to me all morning saying good-bye and asking me when I was leaving. I walked down to the log yard one last time and Big Red, Reema, Olga, and Lena all gave me big hugs. Potarov and Vladislav came into my office after lunch to discuss harvest and road construction plans while I was gone and to say good-bye. Potarov said, "We will miss you, my friend." He then asked, "When are you coming back?" Both men expressed their concern that I might not be returning to Siziman Bay. I reassured them saying, "Why would I not come back? This is my home and where my friends are. I'll be back the second week in January." As he got up to leave, Potarov said, "At the New Year, I will raise a glass of champagne in your honor." "Nikolay," I replied, "I will do the same to you while in Mexico." We gave each other bear hugs and slaps on the back while saying good-bye, and they left. Alone in my office I thought *What a sorry state I've come to when I consider Siziman Bay as home.*

Joe Dill

"Hey *beecht*," I heard Joe call out as he approached, "can't let you leave without a shot of vodka for the road." "Sounds good to me," I replied. We clinked our glasses quietly, saying, "For the road." Joe was around fifty-five years old and a lovable old guy. All the young women in camp thought he was harmless and called him Papa Joe. I occasionally referred to him as my "Grumpy Old Man" because he reminded me of Walter Matthau in the Warner Brothers movie with Jack Lemmon and Ann Margret, *Grumpy Old Men*. Matthau's character was almost a carbon copy of Joe, or vice versa. Both men had similar dark-black hair, relatively large ears, bushy eye brows, large nose, droopy cheeks, and a short chin. Even their posture and shuffling walk was similar, as was their sense of humor. He and I constantly joked around together, and while he claimed that I "made life in camp enjoyable" for him, it is without a doubt that he had helped me get through.

The ride out to Visakogorny was not bad, and I arrived in town in the early evening. We went straight to Lydia's apartment, and I was very surprised when upon meeting me, she gave me a big hug. She quickly boiled up some hot water so I could have some instant ramen noodles and tea for dinner. Nadia, Joe's translator, had come by the apartment on her way back to camp and joined us. Now, we had some good translators working with us at Siziman Bay; however, Nadia was not one of them. She showed no real interest in learning any of the technical terms, either in Russian or English. As a result, she could not be used to assist the mechanics or in any significant business discussions.

One day, after attempting to have what was an important operations discussion with Potarov and having to continuously pause and explain to Nadia what I was talking about, I just gave up. "Nadia, forget it," I had said in frustration and walked away to find Misha. I met Joe on the way to the shop and exclaimed, "Joe, your girl is brain-dead!" He agreed, and the nickname stuck. I had often told Joe that he should fire her and get someone else, but he was too much of a soft heart to do so. She was a nice enough young woman, and Joe felt sorry for her being a single mother always away from her daughter in Khabarovsk.

Not wanting to sleep until on the train, I started to read Tom Clancey's, *Debt of Honor*, leaving the two women alone in the kitchen to chat. I was tired though and fell asleep on the sofa anyway. Brain-Dead woke me up at 1:00 a.m., and thirty minutes later, Lydia accompanied me to the train station and helped purchase my ticket. While standing around waiting for the train to arrive, she asked me again about when I would be coming back. The train arrived on time, and we rushed to my railcar where, after showing the Attendant my ticket and passport, Lydia gave me another big hug and cheek rub while saying good-bye.

I had barely sat down in my compartment when the train started to move on. I sat quietly looking out the window as we rolled on out of town. I couldn't help thinking to myself that not only had I seemed to gain these people's respect, but it felt good that they also seemed to truly consider me their friend. Lydia was able to get me a compartment all to myself this time so that I wouldn't have any hassles with drunks getting on during route this time. Once the Attendant came by again to check my passport and ticket, I quickly fell asleep and didn't wake up until 11:00 a.m. Russian rock-and-roll music played through the intercom all day. I didn't understand the words, but as the kids used to say on *American Bandstand,* "It had a good beat and would be easy to dance to."

I unexpectedly met Dmitry Sharkoff and Vladimir Phillipov at the Shasta Corporation office in the morning. We discussed a few operational issues, but for the most part, Sergei just wanted to express his "desire to work cooperatively" with me. Before they left, Dmitry gave me a picture of his one-month-old granddaughter. I told him, "Good-looking little girl." By the expression on his face, I could clearly see he was one proud grandfather. Placing his hand on my shoulder, he replied, "You can be her honorary American godfather." Even though I continually had difficulty with him on business and operational issues, as a person I really liked the guy and believed he liked me.

Shortly after that, Sergei Golubov stopped by the hotel. He introduced me to Stanislav Khodakov, Assistant to the Head of Migration. Stanislav asked if I—actually if Frontier—would help to finance a trip for some representatives of the Russian Migration Service to Anchorage and Seattle in late January. It became obvious during our discussion that the implied political payoffs for Frontier could be quite significant if they were to contribute. On a personal basis, I supposedly "would not have to worry about ever obtaining a long-term multiple-entry visa." Following the meeting, Sergei drove me to an area outside of the city where a number of people had their dachas. These essentially were small properties roughly five-hundred square meters in size that were used for growing vegetables and fruit. Primarily used on weekends during the summer, some of the sites had small cabins, or maybe more properly described as shacks, on them.

Khabarovsk in the winter is like a fashion show of furs, especially with regard to the women, so late in the afternoon I decided to take a walk and enjoy the scenery. Although coats were made in a variety of styles and from fox or mink, the *shopkas* were primarily mink. By far, the most fashionable shopkas were made from blue mink and were absolutely beautiful. While walking through Lenin Square, I ran into Anna, a young girl I had met a month ago in the Parus bar and had helped to practice her English. She had finished school shortly after we first met and had now moved back to Vladivostok where she was originally from. She happened to be back in Khabarovsk for a couple of days to see friends.

I was surprised that she remembered me. I suppose, though, that it might have had something to do with her now ex-boyfriend becoming extremely upset at her that evening. Anna had spent the entire time talking with me and, not understanding any English, her boyfriend was left out of the conversation—basically being ignored. When his patience finally ran out, he started arguing with Anna and vociferously cussing at me. I didn't understand everything that was being said, but I had learned enough of those words at Siziman Bay to understand the point of what he was making. At the time I thought, what a pistol she was as Anna defiantly defended me, upsetting her boyfriend even more. He had abruptly left the bar without her, and that apparently was the last time she saw him, having broken off their relationship. I remembered at the time thinking the guy was an idiot for leaving such a beautiful girl the way he did, and seeing Anna again just reconfirmed it.

Vladimir and his daughter Tonya came by the hotel the next morning to take me shopping at the Chinese market. The marketplace was a huge outdoor area where people came in every day to set up their tents, tables, vans, or whatever with various items for sale. The majority is clothing, small appliances, and other miscellaneous junk from China. Our goal, with the assistance of Tonya's negotiations, was to purchase a good quality Russian mink fur *shopka* (hat) for me. I was to stand back and keep quiet while Tonya inspected the hats and discussed prices. Only after she was satisfied with a particular hat was I then to come forward and check for proper fitting. Apparently if the vendor realized beforehand that I was an American, the price would have been adjusted upward accordingly.

Later that evening, Vladimir picked me up to have dinner with him and the family at their apartment. Tatyana and Irina were cooking special for me, and dinner consisted of the scallops I'd brought in from Siziman Bay, palmini, various vegetables from Irina's dacha, beer, and wine. They definitely wanted me to eat, because both Irina and Tonya kept refilling my plate. In all, I had a very relaxed evening, although Tonya was wearing the standard short skirt, making it difficult not to focus on her beautiful long legs. The evening's temperature was relatively warm, so Vladimir and Tonya decided to walk back to the Parus Hotel with me. It was a nice walk continuing our casual conversation, but the entire time I was wishing that it was only Tonya accompanying me.

November 23rd, and at 8:45 a.m. the Dalny-Les driver was already waiting outside the hotel to take me to the airport. The scheduled departure was at 11:00 a.m., but the plane was stuck in Vladivostok, and we didn't take off until three o'clock in the afternoon. I didn't have any issues going through Customs and Immigrations, and while being processed, couldn't help again thinking that Russia must have the most attractive Immigration Officers in the world. Fortunately, we didn't have to stop over in Magadan due to bad weather conditions, and this helped to make up for some of our lost time. I sat next to a German girl who had spent ten months south of Khabarovsk doing missionary work. "The first thing I want when I get back to America," she commented, "is a pizza. What about you?" "Me?" I replied. "Right now I'm just happy with my Henry Weinhard's beer and being on a plane going back in time to yesterday."

The meals at Siziman Bay were not the most nutritious or filling, and I was, however, looking forward to getting back to the States and hitting the restaurants. During my first three months in Russia, I lost fifteen pounds, dropping down to 150 which was the same weight I was when I graduated from college twenty-one years earlier. Breakfasts generally alternated between a variation of two eggs or two hot dogs, along with either macaroni without cheese or buckwheat and bread. I had never been a fan of buckwheat and after busting a tooth on a rock, I began doing without.

Lunch usually consisted of either two hotdogs or one piece of chicken, soup which was either *borscht* or *slayanka*, mashed potatoes or macaroni, and bread. After my grandmother passed away when I was a kid, my soups had consisted primarily of Campbell's chicken noodle or vegetable beef from a can. These two soups that the cooks made from scratch each day were delicious and two of the few food items I looked forward to having. Dinners, unfortunately, were not much different than the lunches, with the exception that a simple pastry was usually included.

Sometime in October, however, we began to have turkey for dinner, and I believe every night after that for the next month. We affectionately referred to these as "Bush legs" due to a US administration policy which resulted in huge shipments of turkey legs going to Russia. Turkey had been a pleasant surprise, however, with exception to the manner in which the cooks prepared it. Usually boiled, each drumstick was chopped into two or three pieces using a meat cleaver which resulted in considerable shattering of the bones. After a few of these dinners, we began to make bets on whose piece would have the most bone splitters to deal with. No prize to the winner, just something to help keep the sanity.

I arrived back in the States the morning of Thanksgiving Day, and of course my mother had prepared a huge turkey dinner. Unfortunately, turkey was the last food I wanted, and to be honest, I would have preferred a Big Mac. Before returning to Russia, I took my three kids to Cancun, Mexico, for Christmas. We had a great time snorkeling, horseback riding in the jungle, visiting the Mayan ruins, and just kicking around. My fifteen-year-old daughter out-fished me, catching a barracuda about as long as she was tall. She continues to remind me of this.

Chapter Five

Return to Siziman Bay

Unfortunately my trip out ended all too soon. So on January 8, 1996, I once again boarded the Alaska Airlines flight in Seattle and was on my way back to Russia. On this trip, I had promised Joe that I would stop over in Anchorage to meet and interview one of his friends in Alaska for potential work at Siziman Bay. I had worked in Anchorage for over six years and decided to take the opportunity to meet some of my ex-coworkers for dinner the night before I had to leave. Mike and Sara were a young married couple originally from the Seattle area. Teresa was an attractive woman of Native American descent originally from Arizona who had been my secretary.

After dinner, she and I continued the evening at one of the local bars. My flight to Russia departed at 1:00 p.m. the next day, and we did not return to her house until around nine in the morning, only to find out that her live-in boyfriend had not gone to work that morning. After futilely trying to convince him that nothing wrong was done, he proceeded to sweep the floor with me. At one time, I remember my knee cracking after being thrown over the sofa, bouncing off the coffee table, and landing in the fireplace. Earlier he had found my airline ticket and was threatening to tear it up. I confused him, though. While looking at Teresa, I shrugged my shoulders and said, "Hey, it won't bother me to stay in Anchorage for another week and wait for the next flight." He thought about this for a moment and considered the potential circumstances that could occur if I stayed around. He decided it would be better for me to leave immediately, then he tossed the ticket to me. I didn't argue as I quickly grabbed my bags and waited outside for Teresa. Not much was said on the drive to the airport where, upon arriving, we kissed good-bye, and I painfully limped into the terminal.

Joe and Greg Taylor were waiting for me in the airport bar. I was tired, bruised, and in desperate need of a drink. Joe, having watched me come up the corridor, had already told the waitress at the bar what I needed, and a double Jack Daniels on the rocks was there upon my arrival. I felt like shit, smelled of sex, and by the time I got checked in, we didn't have much time before the flight. Subsequently the interview was brief. Rather bluntly I asked, "Greg, why the hell would you want to go to Russia and work with a couple of misfits like Joe and me?" The reason sounded familiar and his reply was simple, "I just recently got divorced and need to get away, so, why not?" I clinked my glass of Jack Daniels to his glass of beer and said, "If you're crazy enough to go, then you're hired." We bullshitted for a few more minutes, then I paid for our drinks and told Greg we'd see him in Russia in about a month. Joe then helped me through the terminal and onto the plane.

Upon returning to Khabarovsk, I checked into the Parus Hotel. After settling into my room, I went downstairs to the hotel's small, intimate restaurant which served what was referred to as European cuisine. Although the menu selection was limited, it was convenient not to have to go outside to dine. I ordered what had become my favorite appetizer, a small dish of baked scallops covered with mayonnaise and cheese, followed by a cutlet, mashed potatoes, and a beer. I finished dinner and headed to the small room the hotel had converted to a bar.

Usually you would find a mix of foreigners having just arrived or who were about to depart Russia, as well as younger (early twenties) Russians. The choice of alcohol was also limited, which meant that Holston Beer was the primary drink consumed. It really didn't matter though, since the atmosphere was relaxing and the patrons always friendly. Zhenya, the bartender, was a handsome young man and very artistic when it came to making assorted fruit desserts. He had recently graduated from a culinary arts school and although qualified to be a chef, worked at the Parus due to the lack of other options in the city.

Two days later, I arrived in Komsomolsk on schedule at 7:00 a.m. and was met by one of Dalny-Les's drivers waiting outside the station. I was dropped off at the hotel-business center, which was surprisingly cleaner and more comfortable than I had expected. I had just enough time to shave and take a hot shower/bath before getting picked up to go to the office. The cook was waiting to give me breakfast consisting of eggs gooey-side-up, fried ham, and bread and juice. With the exception of lunch and dinner, the remainder of the day on up to 7:00 p.m. was spent in budget meetings. Dinner that evening was a pleasant surprise, with the main feature being a four-inch squid stuffed with Kamchatka crab. I really did miss having a good cup of coffee though. The "American" instant coffee usually provided to us was mixed with powdered milk and an overdose of sugar. In general, it was a very productive day of meetings, and I felt good about the direction everything was going.

After getting back to the hotel, I essentially crashed and slept hard without waking up until 7:30 a.m. the next morning. I felt fresh and got to the office with renewed enthusiasm on concluding discussions on the preliminary budget; then I planned to spend the afternoon shopping. Unfortunately, my enthusiasm was premature and quickly shattered. The Russians were extremely upset about some memo that Cardinal had sent to Bailey, and as a result, Nazarkin, who was currently off somewhere on vacation, refused to allow anyone to discuss any business with us at all. Subsequently, I sat around the office all day accomplishing essentially nothing.

In less than two days I went from an enthusiastic high about the operation to absolute frustration. I didn't know what to think about Frontier, Dalny-Les, Siziman Bay, or Russia in general. Not much had changed since I had been away; it was the same old bullshit as usual from the Russian management there in Komsomolsk. My gut feeling was that Frontier should tell them to fuck off, pull all Americans out, and stop funding all projects until the Russians fell on their asses and decided to truly cooperate. To top it all off, Andrei Chekinkov had gotten his mind set on finding me a Russian wife, thinking that it was not right for me to be alone. I don't know where he got this idea, but that was just what I needed, a woman who couldn't speak English and whose primary objective was to get out of Russia.

The next morning, Chekinkov came by the hotel to get me. "I have very nice lady waiting to meet you," he said. "After some tea at her apartment, we will take you shopping." "Andrei," I answered, "I appreciate your concern about my lack of woman companionship. But I really do have to work today." I added, "At least until noon." I thanked him again and hopped in the car with Cardinal, Pritchard, and Jeff to go to the office. We were hoping to receive a fax regarding any "high level" discussion that went on last night between the folks in Philadelphia and Nazarkin. As expected, but disappointing just the same, nothing had come in.

Since Cardinal wanted to purchase a *shopka* like mine, we decided to take the afternoon off and went to the local flea market to see what we could find for him. Unfortunately for him, his head was too big for all but one shaggy looking hat made from either coyote or possibly dog. I noticed as we walked around that we got a lot of stares and chuckles from the locals, primarily because of the way Cardinal was dressed. What a dork! When we returned to the hotel, Inna told me that Chekinkov had telephoned twice after one o'clock to find out if I had returned. "He's persistent," she said as she chuckled. "Ya," I replied, "I just hope my resistance can outlast his determination."

On the morning of the sixteenth and after two days of wasted time, the Russians finally got the blessing of "his highness" Nazarkin to continue to work with us on the 1996 budget. "You know, John," I commented, "you ought to tell them to stuff it, and they'll have to live with whatever we come up with." "I can't do that," he replied, and by 10:00 a.m. we were back at the table with no apology from the Russians for Nazarkin's bullshit delay. We finalized a draft budget by 6:00 p.m., just in time for me to make it to the train station. The initial figures showed Siziman Bay operations to lose close to $9 million for the year. As I sat in my compartment drinking a beer and watching the countryside roll by, I couldn't help but wonder about Frontier. It was hard for me to understand that Philadelphia would continue to pump money into this project, putting up with the outrageous stunts of Nazarkin, knowing that a profit of any kind could not be expected in the near future. One would think that they were smarter than that.

The train arrived at Visakogorny at 2:45 a.m., and I was immediately driven out to Siziman Bay. The heater in the truck blew exhaust fumes directly into the cab, so we were constantly opening up a window to let fresh air in. There were a number of times that my eyes hurt so bad I couldn't keep them open, and tears would just keep flowing. The temperature outside was minus 30 degrees C or lower which made the trip even more uncomfortable than usual. I'm surprised that my tears didn't immediately freeze to my face, although I did have to pluck an occasional chunk of ice from my moustache. I finally slipped quietly into camp just before 7:00 a.m. and fell asleep in my room until lunch. I was happy to see that my first meal back at camp was not turkey; however it was chicken and, of course, potatoes.

I hadn't noticed my snowmobile around camp. Vladislav Shukalov stopped by the Gulag to welcome me back, and I questioned him about this. Although he didn't come right out and say it, I just figured that the machine was now being used in some remote village located along the rail.

Sabakha, with her tail wagging and a visible grin on her face, came running up to me as I was walking down to the office. I kneeled down to pet her and immediately noticed that her belly had grown. "Oui, you're a *Mama Sabakha*," I exclaimed as she excitedly licked at my face. I had brought back a couple of boxes of Milkbone dog biscuits and pulled one from my pocket. Sniffing at first, she then gently took it from my hand and headed off to check out this unfamiliar new treat.

Chapter Six

Winter, and Back to Insanity

M id-afternoon, I went out to one of the harvest areas with Vladislav and Uyri, a new logging supervisor, to look at the difficulty of the operation. It didn't take me too long to determine what the problem was. "Of course the harvest is difficult," I exclaimed, "you didn't construct the haul road and landing areas as I had designed and instructed you to do before I left camp in November." Uyri commented, "The American trucks would not have been able to climb the road as you identified." I held my temper as I said, "Uyri, I have spent many years designing roads for timber harvest. I can assure you that the trucks would not have had any problem using them as I had located."

Now faced with extremely long skidding distances up a steep hillside, the overall production rates were drastically reduced. To make matters worse, the timber in this particular harvest unit was of relatively low quality and volume per hectare. The area also contained considerable wind-thrown timber from the October storm. Vladislav and Uyri now wanted to quit cutting in this area. When I discussed a number of options with Uyri on how they might improve harvest operations and production, he had a reason for why each one couldn't be done.

"We are not going to be able to reach our production goals," they explained, "and the crew will not get 100 percent of their pay or a bonus this shift." Although I sympathized with them on this issue, I concluded our discussion saying, "You both know damn well that we cannot stop harvesting in this area and go somewhere else. I did not say that it would be easy, but it can be done. You should have followed my instructions. Unfortunately, now you and your crew will just have to live with your error." Looking directly at Uyri I added, "If you do not wish to do this, I will replace you with someone who can and will get the job done!"

I was frustrated with the situation and not paying attention as I walked down the hill toward the truck. I slid on a snow-covered log lying along the skid trail, twisting my knee as I fell to the ground. My knee hurt like hell, and pain shot up into my hip when I attempted to stand. Vladislav and Uyri had already gone off in another direction to meet with the crew. In agony, I laid on the ground thinking, *Damn, first week back in Russia and I'm going to freeze to death.* Crawling to the side of the trail, I cut off a limb from one of the trees to use as a cane. Unable to place any significant weight on my right leg, I slowly limped the rest of the way down the hill to the truck. Back at camp, I wrapped my knee up with an Ace bandage and hobbled down to the log yard. The women were overly concerned about me, and although it didn't ease the pain, I did enjoy the leg massage I received while sitting in the scalers' shack. Later that evening, I brought out a bottle of Jack Daniels and, along with Hubert and Richard, emptied it while watching a movie. That did kill the pain sufficiently to enable me to fall asleep.

Still limping the next day, at least I had a "real" cane to help me along. After lunch, I went out to the woods again with Vladislav and Uyri to look at the other area of operation they were having "difficulties" on. Once again, they had not constructed the roads as I had designed and were now having to skid logs a distance in excess of one kilometer. While doing so, the skidders were bypassing the locations of landing areas that I had identified. "It is impossible to properly locate a road with all the trees standing," Uyri argued. "Besides, the excavator operator followed your ribbon line." I just about came unglued upon hearing this. "Genady," I said as I tried to maintain my temper, "I have yet to swear at a Russian, but I am very close to doing so to Uyri." I turned to Uyri and said, "Please do not insult my intelligence and expertise."

The road had been constructed consistently ten to fifteen feet lower on the hillside than I had located. The critical flat areas I found for switchbacks and landings were missed, resulting in considerable more excavation than there should have been. In places, the blue ribbon I used to identify the centerline of the proposed road could still be seen on the uphill side of the road as built. When I questioned Uyri about this, he arrogantly stated that "the excavator operator did follow your ribbons. This is the road you designed." "Uyri," I calmly replied, "if the operator had followed my ribbon line as he should have, the road would be up there, not down here." He quickly responded, "But he did follow your ribbon; he kept it at his eye level during construction so he would always know how much to excavate." Holding back frustrated laughter, I thought to myself, *Now how in the hell can I argue with this reasoning?* In the United States, road construction operators know that the blue ribbon line is the centerline of the road to be constructed. Never in my wildest dreams did I think that someone would use them as an uphill visual reference as these Russians apparently did.

It was extremely cold on the morning of the twenty-first. At minus 28 degrees C, along with a steady breeze, it was difficult to stay outside for more than fifteen minutes before going inside to thaw out my face. My brown Ford 4x4 pickup was being used by a couple of the Russian mechanics out at the bridge site on the Chichimara River, so I had to use the UAZ "Rooski Jeep." Maybe they didn't think I could handle a stick shift, but everyone seemed to get a kick out of seeing me driving around in it.

I accomplished a real success at the next day's morning meeting and finally got Potarov to agree to start a mandatory maintenance program for the equipment. They now required that each day, one piece of machinery would be brought into the shop so the mechanics could completely go through it.

It was colder than a witch's tit the morning of the twenty-third as the temperature dropped down to minus 38 degrees C overnight. Joe and Brain-Dead arrived into camp about 10:00 p.m. The white Ford pickup that I had sent into Visakogorny to get them came back all smashed up. Apparently some drunk driving a fire truck ran into it and caved in the right side of the bed, tore off one wheel, and damaged the back of the cab. Fortunately the pickup was hit behind the cab, otherwise Lydia, who was sitting in the passenger seat, could have been seriously injured. Joe and I stayed up for a while, having a couple of shots of vodka, relaxing, and "shooting the bull."

I was surprised the next afternoon to find Sasha, our doctor, shit-faced drunk. I had never seen him drink before, and from what I understood, it was the first drink of alcohol that he had had in over eight years. Genady informed me that "Doc found out this morning that his little brother was hit by a car and killed on the way to his birthday party." As I walked away, I thought about how this type of accident was a fairly common occurrence in Russia. I often would see some poor soul sprawled out on the pavement in Khabarovsk or Komsomolsk after being hit by a speeding vehicle.

Andrei Chekinkov came into camp the morning of the twenty-fifth like a Texas tornado. What a character and what energy. Richard slipped on some ice this afternoon on the way to the shop and broke his wrist. He had considerable swelling and was in a lot of pain when I accompanied him to Doc's office. Doc was still drunk and barely able to bandage Richard's wrist. His face was all scratched up and covered with dried blood, apparently from falling down into a crusty snow bank. "Doc," I began saying, "I understand your sorrow, but there are a lot of people here in camp who are relying on you and that you are responsible for in case of emergency. A lot of people have problems they have to face, hardships and heartaches, but alcohol has never been the answer. You need to get yourself together." He just stood there with a glazed look in his eyes and never said a word. After leaving his office, I went to see Chekinkov. "Andrei," I said as I entered his room, "I am concerned about Doc. I appreciate what he must be going through with the sudden loss of his brother, but I'm not happy with having to rely on him while in his current condition." Chekinkov agreed with me and said he would have a talk with him.

The next day, I sent Richard out to Visakogorny to catch the train to Khabarovsk and then a flight back to the States on Sunday. Genady went along to assist in purchasing his tickets, getting him on the right train, and then making it to the airport. His departure left us critically short on mechanics, and fortunately, Hubert agreed to stay on a week longer than previously scheduled. The weather improved throughout the day, warming up to minus 10 degrees C. Since there was no wind, it actually felt quite warm. Doc was still stone drunk today, so Chekinkov sent him back to Komsomolsk. He gave Doc a week to shape up or he'd be fired.

Three days later while Misha and I were driving out to the harvest area, I suddenly mumbled, "What the hell," as I pulled the pickup over to the side of the road. The Freightliner log truck, one of three from the States, was off the road with a 7.6 meter spruce sawlog sticking right through the cab. I asked Misha, "When did this happen? Did you hear anything about this?" Misha's simple reply was, "I don't know, and no." I was turning around to go back to camp when Chekinkov, Potarov, Shukalov, and the truck driver arrived. Nikolay and Vladislav immediately began complaining about the inefficiency of the American trucks. The kid who was driving the truck at the time was blaming the accident on the brakes and steering systems. "Of course the steering and brakes didn't work," I shouted. "The idiot was driving too fast and went out of control on an icy road!" I added, "Look at that log. The stupid kid was lucky he didn't kill himself."

End-of-the-month crew-change day came once again, and as usual, not much work was happening. I was leaning back in my office chair, quietly singing along to Dwight Yokum's "A Thousand Miles from Nowhere" and staring at the wall, when Joe came in from the scale yard. "What's the matter, buddy?" he asked. I replied, "Just thinking about this change in my life and feeling sorry for myself. I don't know. I have this empty feeling, and it's like each day that comes along doesn't fucking matter anymore." "You pot licker," he said. "I don't know why you feel so bad. At least your wife left you for another man; mine left me for a woman! It's cold out and my bones are aching; let's go up to the Gulag and have a warm drink." I reminded him that it was only 10:00 in the morning. "So what, you're the El General here, your boss is on the other side of the world, and we both could use a good drink."

With that I said, "You know, what the hell," and we headed up to the Gulag. I suggested that we microwave up some cognac and water. After our first sip, Joe commented that "it needs something." He quickly went to his bedroom and brought back some brown sugar then added a teaspoon's worth to each drink. We nuked them again in the microwave, and to our pleasant surprise, they tasted pretty good. What started as a mixture of one-third cognac to two-thirds water, ended up being the reverse by noon and subsequently, as with the Russians, our workday was shot. And so, the "Siziman Sludge" came to be.

When I went to the office the next morning, a couple of Russians were huddled at the end of the hall using blowtorches to thaw out pipes. Apparently the furnace had shut off at some time during the night. It was too windy and cold to work outside, so I headed back up to the Gulag for some more coffee. By early afternoon, heat was once again warming up the office building. However, by looking at the numerous black, charred spots on the walls, I was surprised that they didn't burn the place down.

Two days after the Freightliner incident, one of the Timbco feller bunchers caught fire during the night shift. By 6:30 a.m. the next day, Hubert and I were up at the landing site to check out the damage. Fortunately it wasn't anything major, but I told Andrei to have it taken into the shop so the mechanics could check it out thoroughly and clean it up. As we drove away, I mumbled to Hubert, "Russian preventative maintenance plan: wait until equipment either gets smashed or catches fire, then clean up what's left." Even Misha understood the humor in this and laughed with us.

The Russians expected Joe to hand over his passport and visa for them to take into town to be registered. Even though they assured us that the documents would be returned within a week, I adamantly opposed this procedure. I did not feel it was a good idea for an expat to be in Russia without the appropriate documents close at hand, and I had set the policy accordingly. Subsequently, I left camp with Joe on the afternoon of the fourth to go to Komsomolsk and try to straighten out this issue, figuring that it also would give me an opportunity to meet with Phillipov and Chekinkov.

We were about an hour out of Visakogorny when the crew bus broke down, its engine freezing up due to lack of oil. Fortunately for us, the bus was equipped with a small wood-burning stove in the back, otherwise we all would probably have frozen to death. Two of the crew set out on foot for town, and about four hours later, a small Toyota station wagon came to help out. Joe, Tatyana, Nadia, and I were taken to town, arriving around 2:00 a.m., where Grisha then took us to Lydia's apartment for hot coffee, tea, and breakfast. The two girls slept on the larger of the two available beds, and Joe took the smaller "single" bed. Meanwhile, I pushed two chairs together, threw a quilt over myself, and unsuccessfully tried to get some sleep.

Misha and the others arrived in time to meet up with us and catch the 7:00 a.m. train. Joe, Misha, and I slept almost the entire trip. After arriving in Komsomolsk in the afternoon, we immediately went to the office to get Joe properly registered. I also met with Chekinkov and Phillip, their Chief Mechanic, to discuss maintenance and operational issues. It might sound ridiculous, but I finally got them to agree to have all the operators read their appropriate equipment operators manual and sign a document stating they had done so. Also, at my strong suggestion, the mechanics would be placed on a different work schedule than the rest of the crew, so that during major crew-shift changes when the equipment typically is not operating, they could do service work. Later at the apartment, we had to sit around listening to Ron complain about almost everything under the sun. I found it increasingly difficult to be around Ron with his negative attitude toward the Russians, always finding fault with someone else. This was ironic, since it was under his direction that too much money had been spent at Siziman Bay. On top of this, he was the one who essentially lost control of the operations to the Russians.

The next morning was a total waste as the Russians were, to the exclusion of any American input, busy working on the 1996 operating budget. Rather than continue to sit around the office staring at the walls, Joe and I decided to go into town and shop for some food items to bring back to camp.

At 6:40 a.m. the morning of the seventh, one of the Dalny-Les drivers came by the apartment to rush Joe and me to the train station. When we got there, Joe tried to help some little old *babushka* with her three bags, and although I don't know what she said, I do know she really chewed him out! I think she thought that Joe was trying to rob her. Misha showed up just in time for us to catch the 7:20 a.m. train to Visakogorny. "Misha," I asked as he came closer, "what the hell happened to you?" "Oh . . . my Lena and some other friends had been drinking and dancing until just a couple of hours ago. I missed the bus and had to flag down a car to get here." "Well it's a good thing you showed up," I said, "otherwise, I think Joe and I probably would have gotten on the wrong train. By the way, you look like shit."

As usual, the train departed on time, and after getting some blankets from the attendant, we all fell asleep. The heater wasn't working well, so the cabin was quite cold, and I slept with my bald head under the covers to keep warm. When I awoke a couple of hours later, Joe and Misha were still asleep. This trip was the first time I traveled through this stretch of rail during the day. As I sat quietly and watched the countryside go by, I couldn't help but be amazed by the lack of visible signs of wildlife. Kilometer after kilometer would go by without a single track in the snow. Misha finally woke up around one in the afternoon and didn't know whether he wanted a smoke, a beer, or the bathroom. "How about if on the way to the dinner car for a beer," I suggested, "you can stop at the bathroom and then have a cigarette out between the railcars." He moaned, "Oh, I like that, okay." I just chuckled and said, "Let's go." Chuckling to myself as we walked down the aisle, I thought about how much I enjoyed having Misha around.

At Visakogorny, we loaded our things into the crew bus and immediately left for Siziman Bay. I didn't recognize any of the guys on the bus. After about an hour out of town and narrowly missing two loaded log trucks, we stopped to hook on to the crew bus that had died the other night. Our speed was reduced by 50 percent, so it was going to be a long, miserable ride back to camp. Just before reaching the Chichimara River, we came to a steep, icy hill. The driver commented that "the hill is too dangerous," so he had all of us passengers get out and walk while he drove up. I told Joe, "The only thing dangerous about this hill is the driver. Watch what happens."

The driver started his climb and sure enough, about halfway up the hill, he missed shifting the gears, put on his brakes, then slid backward down to the bottom. Fortunately, a fuel truck had come by and after hooking up our bus to it, the three vehicles slowly crawled up and over the incline. During all this time, the rest of us patiently, some less patient than others, stood around freezing our butts off. Not too long after having overcome this obstacle, the driver took a corner too fast and put the bus being towed into the ditch. I decided that we had had enough fun for the evening and told the driver to unhook the bus being towed, and someone could pull it out with a dozer in the morning. We finally made it to the Chichimara River and stopped for what I thought was going to be for just a moment. About ten minutes later, I walked over to one of the crew shacks and found the driver there, sitting and having tea. I chewed him out, then, pointing to the door shouted "now get your ass back on the bus!" We were once again on the road to Siziman Bay, home base for this circus I'd become involved with.

"Fuck Mother Russia and the horse she rode in on!" Only two days back in camp, and I was already past my boiling point and shouting as I walked into my office where Joe was sitting, patiently waiting for me to return from my morning meeting with the Russian managers. "I get lip service from the Russians and zip cooperation from Philadelphia." I continued my ranting, "My title here is General Manager, but that's a fucking joke!" I was becoming increasingly frustrated with the working relationship at Siziman Bay, Komsomolsk, and Philadelphia. The Russian managers excluded me from operational issues to the extent that I let them, and since there were more than ten of them per shift and only one of me, it was next to impossible to keep on top of everything. "Well, Joe," I said, "I'm tired of the cooperation being only Americans to Russians and not getting something back. So, tonight, fuck 'em!"

The American mechanics at Siziman Bay would often put in twelve-plus hours of work per day, seven days a week. After dinner that evening, I was sitting in the Gulag kitchen with Hubert and Karl Jansen complaining about this and the lack of cooperation from the Russians. "Tonight we're going to stir things up a little," I told the both of them. "If anyone comes to you after seven o'clock and asks for assistance, tell them you can't do it unless I authorize it." As if right on cue, and within minutes after I said this, Hubert was informed that one of the Hahn Harvesters had broken down and asked if he could go check it out. It literally blew the Russians' minds when they were told no, and that they had to ask me first. Lydia and Uyri found me in the office and excitedly began to confront me regarding this new policy. "The mechanics have already put in twelve hours of work today," I calmly explained. "In addition, why should we cooperate with you, when I get no cooperation back?" A very heated argument ensued, and when I still refused, they rushed off to complain to Potarov.

I closed up my office, walked back to the Gulag, and found Hubert and Karl still in the kitchen watching a John Wayne movie. "Hubert," I said, "would you mind going out to the Hahn and helping the crew out? Uyri and Lydia still think I won't let you go, but we do have a responsibility and obligation to Philadelphia to help keep production up." "Sure," he replied, "no sweat. I'll take Misha with me," and off he went. Neither the Russian partners nor the Philadelphia office ever really appreciated how good the mechanics were that we had at Siziman Bay.

My throwing a "riggin' fit" the previous night apparently paid off. Following their usual 8:30 a.m. radio call to the Komsomolsk office, the Russian managers were extremely pleasant and cooperative with me. Later when Joe walked into my office, he commented that "according to the grapevine, the Russians actually do respect you," adding sarcastically, "although I don't know why." "You asshole," I replied. He continued by saying, "From what I gather, they appreciate your patience and that you have not forced your authority on them. Word is that they now realize you can be pushed only so far, and that you have no problem taking an issue to the limit. They also apparently got the message today that you do, in fact, have the backing from both Philadelphia and Komsomolsk." All I could say was, "We'll see."

The next morning I was walking from the Gulag down to the office when I noticed Genady and Doc come out of the Doc's office wearing only towels around their waists. Curious, I turned to walk over to say good morning to them. They were filling up buckets with water when I got there, so I asked what they were up to. Genady told me that it "was good for your health to pour cold water over your body" and asked if I wanted to join them. I quickly replied, "No fucking way," adding, "You guys are crazy!" They continued to try and convince me as I was walking away. Then, completely naked in subzero temperature, they began to dump water over each other's head. Three days later, both the Doc and Genady were stuck in bed with high fevers.

At the camp, there were separate hours set up for the men and women to use the banya. One afternoon, Lena, one of the young log scalers, came to me and invited me to the banya that evening. I asked Misha if she was kidding. He wasn't sure, but thought she was and said since she was such a tease, why not call her bluff. After dinner that night, I took Misha and headed down to the banya. We knocked and soon Big Red opened the outer door. She asked what we were doing there and, when Misha told her about Lena's invitation, she essentially told us to get the hell out of there and slammed the door shut. With that, I suggested to Misha that since we had the vodka already, we should grab some bread and sausages from the kitchen and head down to the beach to make a fire and get drunk. He replied *pachcheemoo neyht* (why not), and we did just that.

I left Siziman Bay on the morning of the thirteenth, and three days later arrived in Seattle. I was there in part to meet up Cardinal, Nazarkin, Phillipov, Chekinkov, and Sharkoff, and to accompany them to Eugene, Oregon on the twenty-second for the Pacific Logging Conference. Throughout the trip, Cardinal continued to prove what an idiot he was, and on more than one occasion, reconfirmed his stupidity to me. God how I wished I could have worked with someone who had some brains.

On the afternoon of the twenty-fifth, I departed from Seattle on Alaska Airlines bound for Anchorage to connect with an Aeroflot flight that went on to Khabarovsk. Unfortunately, but not unexpectedly, the departure from Anchorage was delayed due to the Aeroflot plane coming in late from San Francisco. The flight to Khabarovsk was full, and with the exception of myself and three other Americans, all the passengers were Russian. The seating was "open," and I slowly made my way down the aisle, politely asking people if I could sit in a vacant seat next to them. Tired of either not being understood or more likely just being ignored, I finally mumbled "fuck you" and climbed over the guy sitting in an aisle seat so that I could get to the vacant window seat beyond him.

I slept virtually the entire six-hour flight, and upon clearing customs at 12:30 a.m., walked into the lobby with one less bag than I had checked in with. I fortunately found one of the airport managers and got him to understand my situation. We wandered around the airport, and upon entering the cargo building, came upon one employee opening a large box of flowers and giving a bouquet of roses to each of two women with him. Needless to say, they were extremely surprised to see us, but the manager just smiled at them and we continued our search. We finally located my baggage, and the Dalny-Les driver dropped me off at the Parus Hotel around 2:00 a.m.

Although I was told I'd be picked up at noon, the driver came by the hotel for me at 10:00 a.m. Instead of the train, today we were taking one of the new Ford pickup trucks for what turned out to be a five-hour drive back to Komsomolsk. It was a beautiful sunny day as we left the city limits, Russian rock music blaring over the stereo system. The road and forested terrain were similar to areas north of Wasilla, Alaska. We passed through three police checkpoints along the way. We were directed to pull over at one of these where, following a brief conversation, I had to show them my passport. Along the way, I noticed that at one point the road had widened into what appeared to be four lanes that were arrow straight for quite some distance. I thought it curious that the right-of-way clearing had also become considerably wider than usual. I questioned the driver about this, and through broken English and hand gestures learned the reasoning for this. Apparently this portion of road was also designed as an emergency landing strip for the MIG fighter jets stationed at Komsomolsk.

Misha had come into camp on the first bus bringing in the change of crews on March 1st and found me sitting in the Gulag kitchen having a beer. He stood at the door and said, "Hello Paul, I got something to show you," then asked me to come to his room. After closing the door, he pulled a quart jar of clear liquid out of his duffle bag. Holding it up for me, he smiled and said, "This is *summagon*." "It's not purified yet, and I need you to help." "What do we need to do?" I asked. He handed me a small bag of granular coal, saying, "We need to filter it through this." Misha rolled up a piece of newspaper into the shape of a cone and partially filled it with some black granules. When he opened the jar of summagon, he quickly moved to open the window and let the smell escape. "I don't want people to know that we have this here in camp," he said. While pouring the brew into the newspaper cone, some of the liquid spilled onto the floor. "Shit," Misha said, "that is going to be a problem tomorrow morning." Once finished with the filtering process, we put the jar into our refrigerator to let it settle.

The next day after dinner, Misha, Joe, and I headed up to the Gulag to sample Misha's concoction. Before going into the kitchen lounge, we stopped by Misha's room to look at the hole in the carpet where we had spilled some of the brew the night before. Chuck and Hubert were already up at the Gulag, and being up for the challenge agreed to join us. Joe placed five shot glasses on the table, and Misha proudly filled them with his home brew. We each grabbed a glass and raised them in toast to "Misha's summagon." Joe shouted, "Yeeoowh!" Gasping, I whispered, "Lord this stuff burns." Misha laughed and said, "Watch this." He grabbed a tablespoon, placed it on the table, and poured some of the brew into it. He then flicked his cigarette lighter and touched its flame to the spoon, causing the liquid to immediately light up. The bluish-hued flame continued for a few minutes until the summagon was completely burned off. "All right!" I exclaimed, "Guys I think we just found a solution to getting the four-wheeler started in the mornings!"

We had hired a crew from the Ukraine to help increase our harvest production through the balance of the winter season. A week after they had arrived, I went out with Big Red to where they were working, to check on log quality. I was also interested in general just to see how their operations were proceeding. All cutting of trees was by hand using an interesting Russian chainsaw that was fashioned in such a manner that a person didn't have to bend down to cut the tree at ground level. The yarding of tree-length logs to the landing area was done by using one of the three beat-up looking Russian TT4 Track Skidders provided by Dalny-Les for them to use. At best, they were only able to use one at a time because there seemed to always be one at the landing under repair and another broken down in the woods. As it turned out, the current broken-down machine was being towed onto the landing as we drove up. Although I took some photographs and video while there, the Ukrainians did not like me doing so and would always turn away. I commented on this to Misha on the way back to camp, and he said it was probably because it was illegal for them to be there.

The next day was March 8th, a very special national holiday in Russia when even the banks close. International Woman's Day is a time for celebrating and expressing appreciation toward women. The women in camp were going to have a party that evening down in the cookhouse and invited me and Misha to join them. I think this was in part due to the fact that I had the best stereo sound system in camp. When I entered the cookhouse at nine o'clock, the ladies had all but one table pushed up against the walls to make room for a dance floor. Various salads, two cakes, a variety of chocolates, and seven bottles of champagne were already set on the table.

This celebration was an unexpected event for me, and fortunately I had a bottle of champagne and a bottle of cognac in stock that I could contribute to the festivities. Misha and I popped the tops off a couple of bottles and filled everyone's glass with champagne. I raised my glass and with a toast "to the beautiful women of Russia, especially the ones here at Siziman," the party began. As difficult as you could imagine it was to dress up and look beautiful while at a remote logging camp, the two cooks, Marina and Natasha, as well as Reema did fairly well for themselves. The three of them had obviously spent some time during the day fixing up their hair. In addition to the lipstick that no Russian woman ever goes without, they wore eye liner and blush.

International Woman's Day Waltz

After a while, Reema asked if I knew how to waltz, to which I replied, "It's one of my favorites." With a smile, she shyly asked me if I'd dance one with her. I looked through my CDs, put on Tracy Lawrence's "Dancin' to Sweet 17," then took Reema's hand and the dance floor was ours. As we glided around the floor, the other girls looked on, clapping when the music finished. Reema curtsied, and I returned her gesture with a bow. Later in the evening, I put on another waltz figuring it was my turn to ask her to dance. I was unaware at the time, but apparently the women had already determined that I was to be Reema's man, and from that point in time, I was hands-off for everyone else.

The unfortunate thing about this holiday is that it also gives the men in Russia another reason to drink just as much, and probably more than the women do. At Siziman Bay, on this particular evening it proved to be fatal. About midnight, I was informed that a crew member out on one of the logging sites was killed. Apparently one of the skidder operators, for some unknown reason, was trying to get a chunk of wood away from the log processor. The operator of the Hahn Harvester, not seeing him in the darkness, processed a log, then kicked it off the machine. The log caught the guy in the chest, knocking him down and into the pile of other logs. I understand that he only survived for about two minutes, having broken his back and neck. In the morning, everyone in camp was already contributing money to give to his family. I was once again impressed with the Russians' genuine caring that they expressed toward each other. None of these people had much themselves but would freely give what they could to help out their fellow comrades.

Three days later, I left camp at 8:00 in the morning in one of the 1995 Ford trucks that I had finally wrangled out of the Komsomolsk office. Coming in from Visakogorny, the truck arrived late, but at least it signaled that the road was drivable. Potarov told the driver that if he didn't get me to the train to Khabarovsk on time, he would lose his job. Knowing how Russians normally drive (they'd do well on the Baja 500), I said good-bye to everyone, and climbed in the cab, whispering a silent prayer as I did. It was an absolutely beautiful sunny, spring day, and in the new extended cab pickup, the ride for once was quite comfortable. After we cleared the pass, the driver put the pedal to the metal, and I tightened up my seat belt. Fortunately, we were driving during daylight hours, so visibility was good.

When we got past the Tumnin River, I began to notice a considerable amount of animal tracks in the snow. I don't think this driver had ever seen a moose before, because when we did, he almost drove off the road while turning his head back to look as we passed on by. Unfortunately, the next moose we saw was closer to the road, and this time the driver slammed on the brakes, causing the pickup to smack into the snow berm off the edge of the road. Other than wanting to strangle the guy, my only thought was, *Damn!*

He put the transmission in reverse gear and punched the pedal to the floor, which of course caused the tires to spin and dig deeper into the snow. He tried the same technique again, and I quickly reached over and pulled the keys out of the ignition before he made matters worse. I got out of the cab, grabbed a shovel from the back of the truck, and started digging a track behind each wheel. I then broke off some branches from the bushes, placing a few within the tracks. Motioning for the driver to do the same, I continued to dig our way out. Once I had tracks established for each tire and sufficient brush within them for added traction, I got into the driver's seat and slowly backed out onto the roadway.

I looked at my watch. We had wasted roughly forty-five minutes, and I was now really worried about making it to Visakogorny in time. I pointed to my watch, showing the driver the time of the train's departure. He gave me the thumbs-up sign, and with a big smile said, "*Neyht problem!*" We saw two more moose and one elk along the way, but the driver didn't flinch a muscle on either occasion and never took his foot off the gas pedal. When we arrived at Visakogorny, I had to run to get on the train as the attendants were pulling up the steps. I climbed up, and as he was running alongside the railcar, the driver threw my bags up to me.

The train left Visakogorny at noon, on time as usual. Four hours into the twenty-hour ride to Khabarovsk, as I stared out the window, drinking one of the beers I purchased from the restaurant railcar, I couldn't help but reflect on life at Siziman Bay. A lot had happened, yet nothing much had happened since my return to Russia. During January while in Khabarovsk, Joe Dill had slipped on an icy sidewalk and hurt his shoulder. Despite the numerous acupuncture treatments given to him by Doc, he still had not improved, so I finally forced him to go back to the States and have it looked at. When I had spoken with him the previous day, he had just returned home from the doctor's clinic and seemed to be in good spirits. Fortunately, his shoulder was not broken, but there was a separation of the ligament and the area had become infected. He still planned on returning to Russia later in the week after he moved his youngest daughter up to Homer, Alaska.

Joe sounded happy now that he would again have a place to call home and "somewhere to go back to" on his trips out. This left just me with nowhere other than Siziman Bay to call home. Joe was about the kindest, most gentle old man that I have ever met. Having a natural comic wit, able to crack a joke in just about any situation, he was also our "fashion disaster" at camp. Typical morning attire into the Gulag kitchen for Joe would be a pair of Bermuda shorts over blue long underwear and a blue thermal long-sleeve shirt under a T-shirt. To complement this, he would usually wear white or gray wool socks and "Archie" style sandals.

The past winter had been hard on Joe, and he had become increasingly desperate for some woman to love him. Of the three women in camp that he had been interested in, the two Natashas flirted and joked around with him constantly, but they wouldn't take him seriously. He was really hung up on Big Red, but she had ticked him off big time a couple of weeks earlier. I'm not sure what happened, but she hurt his feelings somehow, and now the two of them hardly spoke to each other. Marina, one of the cleaning ladies and his other interest, was apparently madly in love with one of the Hahn operators and planned to get married. Joe started to hit the brandy quite often after the episode with Natasha, and I also think due to the pain in his shoulder. I hoped that this current trip out to the States would help him regroup his thoughts.

Genady had left camp on the seventh to translate for some high-level Russian-Chinese commission regarding the disputed international boundary location south of Khabarovsk. He and I had struck up what I felt to be a true friendship, not just an American employer—Russian interpreter relationship. I firmly believed that with his expertise, he could have done much better for himself than there at Siziman Bay, but he planned to return on April 1st. Genady was a gentle man, even-tempered, and very little seemed to discourage or upset him. He appeared to be in love with Reema and had now taken it upon himself to "end me of my misery of being alone." I figure the recent spring weather had affected him, as it did Joe, and this sudden self-imposed responsibility toward my best interests would pass during his trip away from camp. At least I hoped so!

Reema's daughter, Anya, started work as a scaler on the first of March. She was an extremely beautiful, petite young woman, twenty-four years old, with a five-year-old daughter. Her ex-husband was in prison for what reason I did not know. When Anya smiled or laughed, she tried so hard not to open her mouth because of her two missing front teeth. Joe would always greet her in the morning, saying something like, "How's my I wanna lay Anya this morning?" Not knowing English, she would just giggle back at him. Sveta was late coming back to camp, having just gotten out of the hospital on the sixth. She had such a pleasant, bubbly personality and was a real kick to have around the office. Lena slipped on the ice the other day and broke her wrist. She didn't want to go home, so for two days I gave her ibuprofen for the pain then finally convinced her to go see a doctor back in Visakogorny. I recently learned, and this confirmed my suspicions, that Lena had had a real rough experience with men. Apparently she saw a lot of both verbal and physical abuse by her father toward her mother and perhaps herself as well. A friend she had, as recently as last November, had broken her nose twice, which explained why it was not straight.

Sometimes it was difficult not to think of the miserable life these people went back to each time they left camp. Then there was Natasha, or *mylinky* (little) as Joe calls her. Big Red's daughter, she had beautiful auburn hair, blue eyes, and was a spitfire to her mother. They had at times gotten into some real intense fights which was probably why they ended up working separate shifts. While Sveta had the meek little-mouse characteristic that allowed people to walk all over her, Natasha didn't take flak from anybody. Nadia, Joe's interpreter, arrived back in camp last night having escorted Greg Taylor in from Khabarovsk. Divorced, with a ten-year-old daughter, she apparently had also been unlucky with the men in her life. From what I understood, she had recently fallen in love with some American who promised her the world then left without even saying good-bye. It had taken a long time for her to get comfortable around me, and I was surprised when she gave me a big hug upon saying hello. She could be difficult at times, which was what she always said about me, but she was usually in good spirits. I just wished she was a better translator.

Misha

Misha (Mikhail) Kuchin was not only my favorite translator, but over the previous six months had become a good friend. Twenty-three years old, Misha was good-natured, loved music (especially the Beatles), and was simply trying to enjoy life. Constantly asking me to explain what various English words or phrases meant, his desire to improve his communication skills was unending. He also showed a keen interest in learning the operational and business issues involved in timber harvesting and shipping. He and some of his friends in Komsomolsk wanted me to spend an evening at their local disco before I went back to the States. I figured I'd probably try to do this, as it sounded like it might be fun. So, these were my "kids" here at Siziman Bay. Maybe I was suffering from illusions of grandeur, but I'd like to think that at least with these people I was making a positive difference in their lives.

The train arrived at the station in Khabarovsk at eight o'clock the next morning. A Dalny-Les driver was waiting to take me to the Parus Hotel. Since it was still early, and I was not looking forward to seeing Cardinal, I decided to have breakfast in the hotel restaurant first. Ludmilla at the front desk had mentioned to Phillipov where I was, and he stopped in to have coffee with me before going up to Cardinal's room. Cardinal was catching the afternoon flight back to the States, so the meeting was relatively short and left me wondering why I even had to make the trip. Once he was gone, I spent the afternoon walking around town looking for souvenirs and stocking up on booze for camp. I had nowhere else to go, so I hung around the Parus bar that evening until it was time to catch the 10:00 p.m. train back to Komsomolsk.

Chekinkov met me at the station the next morning and informed me we were going to drive to Visakogorny in one of the Ford pickup trucks. Galina, Dalny-Les's Chief Accountant, was to be traveling with us, supposedly to perform an audit at Siziman Bay. I say "supposedly" because I think Andrei was still trying to set me up with a "good Russia woman." The initial twenty-seven or so kilometers of road out of Komsomolsk is on the same paved highway taken to Khabarovsk. Shortly after the village of Selikino, the route turns east onto a two-lane gravel road for roughly forty kilometers to the village of Snezhney. At this point, the road becomes not much more than a one-lane path for roughly ninety kilometers, and for the most part, traverses alongside the railroad. Approximately fourteen kilometers out of Visakogorny, the road once again becomes gravel, two lanes, and in reasonably good condition. Along the way and at the top of one of the mountain passes, we came to an army outpost. While Andrei dealt with the army guard to gain clearance to proceed, I decided to use the outhouse and get rid of some of the beer I had been drinking along the way. I opened the door and stood looking at a large pile of frozen urine and shit extending up and out of the hole. Definitely gross, but at least it didn't smell, so I quickly added my contribution and left. Thankful that I only had to piss, I returned to the truck shaking my head in disbelief.

Early on the morning of March 15th, Sergei Phillipov telephoned from Komsomolsk. Alexie Nazarkin was in Moscow and apparently on a drunk. Following Nazarkin's directive, Sergei ordered all logging stopped at Siziman Bay but did not inform the Russian managers why. Only the Ukrainian logging crew was allowed to continue cutting timber, but no logs were to be hauled to the sort yard. Construction on the bridge at the Chichimara River was also allowed to continue. Other than for these operations, no equipment was to be turned on. Until further notice from Nazarkin, the Russian personnel were to be kept busy by cleaning up the camp area. From what I later found out, he apparently got upset at the folks in the Philadelphia office when they wouldn't wire him $60,000 for a plane ticket back to Komsomolsk and who knows for what else.

Later in the day, I met with Uyri, Vladislav, and Lydia to develop a maintenance schedule for the equipment in order to take advantage of the unexpected shutdown of operations. We also discussed the need, and I got them to agree to continue the sort yard operations. Over the next two days, the logs in the yard which were not previously scaled and sorted were "unofficially" processed. To many people, this might not sound like much, but their agreeing to do this was a significant show of confidence in me and their willingness to cooperate. It also was a lot for me to ask of them. If Nazarkin had found out about it, the three of them would probably have been punished and/or fired.

Two days later, I was sitting in the office when Lydia and Vladislav got another telephone call from Phillipov in Komsomolsk. Their voices became very excited, and when they turned to look at me, I could see a look of shock in their eyes. Vladislav hurriedly left the room and moments later returned with Misha. I then learned that Nazarkin had now ordered all of the Americans out of not only Siziman Bay, but Russia as well. "Vladislav," I said, "I do not work for that drunken son-of-a-bitch Nazarkin. I hope you two have someone other than my friends try to escort me out, because it will have to be at gunpoint." Still on the telephone, Vladislav informed Sergei of my reply. Lydia looked at me and said, "Paul, we will walk out together." I wrapped my arm around her shoulder, then giving her a hug I smiled and replied, "*Neyht*, I'm staying here in camp!" Vladislav hung up the telephone and said, "Phillipov wants us to do nothing until he arrives in camp tomorrow, so that you and he can discuss the situation." "Sounds good to me," I said, "now let's go up to the Gulag and have some choot-choots. You two need to relax."

Sergei and Andrei arrived in camp around nine o'clock the next evening. I had already gone to bed, but since they were anxious to meet with me, I got back up. I found the two of them waiting in Andrei's room with a variety of snacks, beer, and vodka set out on a small table. Both men stood up when I entered the room, giving me big bear hugs as we greeted each other. We started the evening with a toast to friendship, but I knew what they really wanted to discuss. Eventually the conversation got around to Nazarkin's directives. "Paul," Sergei started, "I really do not want to do this, but I must follow Alexie Nazarkin's order." "Sergei," I replied, "I consider you and Andrei not only as business partners but as good friends as well. I can appreciate your position, but I really don't understand."

Andrei grabbed my arm, looked straight into my eyes, and pleaded, "Paul, we need you to leave camp and go to Khabarovsk until this situation is over." "I'll compromise," I said. "If I have not heard from the Philadelphia office by 9:00 a.m. tomorrow morning instructing me to leave, I will have the mechanics pack up and leave at Sergei's direction." However, I stressed to the both of them that I was in Siziman Bay to work with them and that "I do not want to be difficult, but I work for Philadelphia. As I said before, if you attempt to force me to leave, it will have to be at gunpoint." Then half joking I added, "I hope it will not be one of you doing the escorting." Sergei quickly changed the subject in an attempt to ease the tension. We drank, joked, and generally bullshitted as friends normally do until after midnight. At one o'clock in the morning, I telephoned the Philadelphia office to inform them of the situation, then, thoroughly exhausted, went to bed.

Later that morning after catching a few hours of sleep, I grabbed a cup of coffee then walked down to the office. In the machine was a fax which simply stated, "The order to leave is canceled." However, due to the time difference in Moscow, Phillipov did not hear from Nazarkin until later in the day. During their morning conference call, Sergei had told the Komsomolsk personnel that the Americans in camp were packed and ready to leave. This of course was not true, but he had done this to defuse any questions that might have come up. So by late afternoon, it was once again business as usual at Siziman Bay, and harvest operations began with the evening shift.

After dinner a couple of days later, I drove out to the logging area with Big Red to "educate" the operators on improving their cutting and sorting of logs. While there, she made one operator put five logs back onto the Hahn and re-cut them. Once I explained to Natasha why I wanted to do certain things in a certain way, she really took control and rode the operators hard to make sure they'd perform. In this particular case, the reason was why it was more profitable to take a 7.6 meter #3 grade log and cut it into a 3.8 meter #1 grade log and a 3.8 meter pulp log. She was such a kick to watch, and all I needed to do was sit back as she'd chew ass.

The next morning, she bet me a case of champagne that the ice would not be out of the bay and log shipments would not start before May. "Natasha," I said, "I'll take that bet, but if I win you and the other girls will have to help me drink it!" She laughed and said "*Conyeshna,*" which means "of course" and walked out of the room.

Takahara and Kikuma, also with Osika Corporation, had come in by helicopter with Cardinal and Phillipov the day before. They now walked into my office as Natasha was leaving. While in the middle of our negotiations, I heard Cardinal in the hallway preparing to leave camp. He had essentially ignored me and the rest of the Americans during the past two days, and I was becoming increasingly ticked off about it. I don't know if it was because he thought he was too important to deal with the specific details of day-to-day operations, or if he was just too stupid to understand.

I jumped up from my chair as he was walking out the front door and shouted, "John, what the hell is going on here? Where are you going? You know damn well that I need to discuss some issues with you before you leave!" "Okay, all right," he replied, "but Phillipov wants to leave early, so we need to do it right now." "Damn," I mumbled under my breath. Embarrassed with the situation, I turned and said, "Takahara-san, I apologize for this interruption, but I really need to talk with Cardinal before he leaves. Can we continue our meeting in about an hour?" "Of course, Paul-san," he replied, and he and Kikuma departed. Thirty minutes later and without discussing much of anything in detail, Cardinal abruptly said, "I gotta go," and left my office without even saying good-bye. I leaned back in my chair and thought, *How in the hell is this operation going to survive with a fucking idiot like that supposedly in charge?*

I caught the 7:00 p.m. train from Komsomolsk on April 2nd and upon my arrival in Khabarovsk the next morning, was met by the Dalny Resources Company's driver. We drove to the Parus Hotel where, at the front desk, Ludmilla expressed her relief in seeing me. Someone apparently had told her that I would be arriving at five o'clock in the morning and with a big smile, she greeted me saying, "Mr. Tweiten, it is so good to see you. I was so worried that something terrible had happened to you." I thanked her for her genuine concern for me and added that "it is always so nice to see your smiling face when I come here." I gave her my passport to register, saying, "By the way, I like the dress you are wearing, it looks very beautiful on you." Her smile widened as she handed me the room key. All the employees there at the hotel knew me on sight by now and always greeted me with genuine smiles. Everyone—the doorman, cleaning ladies, waitresses, and receptionists—were very pleasant toward me, and they were always willing to help. Although I had slept the entire way from Komsomolsk to Khabarovsk, when I got up to my room I flopped down on the bed and crashed for another two hours.

I stopped by the Shasta office briefly to say hello to Olga. About five feet six inches in height, she had soft, brown hair cut to chin length, beautiful brown eyes, and her curves proportionately in all the right places. Like many of the women in Khabarovsk, Olga usually wore her skirts short showing off her gorgeous, long legs, and today was no exception. She had such a sweet personality, was always pleasant, and never failed to greet me with a big smile. Not only was Olga quite attractive physically, she also had a soft-spoken voice and cute accent. Just hearing her voice would melt away any stress you might have had.

With time on my hands, I decided to walk around Khabarovsk and check out some stores for souvenirs. Eventually I made it down to the public marketplace, which was extremely busy. People were chaotically scurrying about everywhere. Wearing my fur shopka and speaking only Russian, which meant I spoke very little, I didn't get hassled as an American by anyone. No one stared at me like they would with Cardinal in his shaggy dog skin shopka. Later that night, I stopped into the Parus bar and had a few drinks with one kid, I think about twenty-one years old, that I'd seen in there a couple of times before. During our conversation, I learned that he used to be a dancer and had toured in the United States, Japan, Korea, and China. Unfortunately, his knee gave out on him so he was forced to quit and was now back in the university studying for his business degree. Like many of the younger Russians, he was enthusiastic and very optimistic about the future of Russia.

It was 11:50 a.m. on April 4th and if the flight attendants could have gotten the group of Boy Scouts, most of whom were adults, to sit down, the Alaska Airlines DC-10 would have left the terminal on time. The folks at Shasta wanted to see me once I got back to the States to discuss my taking the position with them. However, my primary objective during this vacation was to disappear for a while at a dude ranch in Colorado Rocky Mountains. After that, I intended to spend some quality time with my kids back in Michigan. I was also hoping that I could decide what I wanted to do regarding my employment future. Sometimes I got so frustrated with the Siziman Bay operations, primarily with certain individuals in Philadelphia that it was all I could do to just get up in the morning. Plus, working twelve to fourteen hours a day, seven days a week—I was flat tired! Other times though, the Russians would hit me with some off-the-wall, from-the-heart comment that kept me committed to making the Siziman Bay project work. During a meeting in Komsomolsk a few days earlier, both Phillipov and Chekinkov expressed how much they liked working with me, and that they were afraid of what would happen if I were to leave. Of course, then I met with Cardinal briefly the same morning, and that just reconfirmed what a jerk he was.

Spring

M y vacation was over, and I was back in the hotel at SeaTac on May 3rd when my cell phone rang. I answered; it was Joe calling from Siziman Bay. "Hey you pot-licker. Are you ready to come back home?" "You old fart," I replied. "What the hell do you think?" After giving me an update on what was happening, he told me, "I heard Potarov is coming back to camp; should be here by the time you return." My response was quick, "Damn, must mean that he was denied his heart surgery." Joe said, "I think you're right, and from what Genady tells me, the ole boy really needs it in order to live much longer." "I can't believe they're sending him back to all the stress at Siziman Bay," I replied. "I sure hope it isn't during one of our discussions that he has his next heart attack. Damn it, Joe, I just can't believe it."

Joe Basil stopped by the hotel in the evening to talk about Siziman Bay, my short-term goals, John Cardinal, and the manager's position with Shasta based in Khabarovsk. "I'm extremely interested in the position," I told him, "but I don't think the timing is right for me to leave the Siziman operations right now." He agreed, adding that "the operation seems to be at a turning point, and it is probably best for you to stay on and see it through the next couple of months. I'm not in a big hurry on the Khabarovsk position anyway, so we can wait." After he left, I couldn't help but wonder what it was that everybody thought that I did that was so special. I didn't feel like I accomplished a whole lot.

The Alaska Airlines flight arrived at Khabarovsk relatively on time the afternoon of the fifth, and it was nice not to see any snow on the ground. After clearing Customs and Immigrations, I plowed through the crowd waiting in the lobby and past the numerous guys asking, "Taxi? Taxi?" Vasily, one of the Dalny-Les drivers, and Galena, their Khabarovsk office translator, met me outside. Before dropping me off at the Parus Hotel, they took me to the train station to purchase my ticket to Komsomolsk the following night.

I was exhausted by the time we made it to the hotel, but not wanting to sleep yet, I decided to hit the bar and unwind from the long flight. I wasn't feeling up for vodka, so I requested a Holston beer then sat down at one of the small tables. I was on my second beer when a middle-aged woman approached me and asked if I was an American. I replied that I was, and she immediately sat down. She informed me that she was an English teacher and the young woman sitting with her was one of her students. "Would you mind sitting and talking with us?" she asked. "I was hoping to have her practice her English with someone other than myself." I was tired and not really in the mood for company, but after one quick glance toward her beautiful, young blonde companion, how could I resist?

As I approached their table, I couldn't help looking at this young woman's gorgeous legs, her short miniskirt exposing an enticing amount of thigh. I sat down, extended my hand across the table to hers, and introduced myself. Khabarovsk has more than its fair share of beautiful women, and this one was no exception. With her tight-fitting light-blue sweater accentuating her ample-sized breasts, I thought even Hugh Hefner would have considered her Playmate material. I quickly offered to buy them a drink and signaled for Zhenya.

Apparently Ludmilla had been instructing Lena for about one year but was frustrated because the opportunity to communicate with foreigners in Khabarovsk was limited. Lena was soft-spoken, probably due to her self-confessed lack of confidence in speaking English. She had a cute little accent though, and as I looked into those beautiful blue eyes, I couldn't help thinking how nice it would have been if Ludmilla were to leave. I don't really remember how we came upon the subject, but at some point during our conversation, Ludmilla told me that Lena was only eighteen years old. I was both shocked and amazed. Back in the States, this gorgeous young girl would easily have passed as being in her mid-twenties. I was disgusted with myself. There I was thinking how nice it would be to get her up to my room, and she was not much older than my daughter. Shortly after learning this, I finished off my beer. Then using the excuse of being tired after the long trip, I said good night and went up to my room.

Everyone in Russia had just come off a three-day holiday called May Day. In a few more days on the ninth, there was another one called Victory Day in celebration of the end of the Patriotic War (WWII) in Europe. Russia seemed to have more excuses for holidays and not working than I could have ever imagined. Nadia, Joe's translator, came by the hotel in the morning to let me know she wouldn't be traveling with me to Siziman Bay. I hardly recognized her when I first saw her come in. This was the first time I had seen her in a dress, high heels, fashionable jacket, and wearing makeup. She actually looked quite attractive.

On the train back to Komsomolsk the next evening, I ended up with one other person in the cabin with me and, of course, he snored. In addition, I don't think they had adjusted the heating system on the train from the winter settings, and as a result, the cabin was extremely warm. I stripped down to only my briefs and covered myself with only the bedsheet, but I was still sweating like a son-of-a-gun. The heat combined with the continuous snoring from my traveling companion for the night, made it difficult to get a decent sleep.

On the evening of May 7th I boarded the train from Komsomolsk to Visakogorny with Lydia and her boyfriend, Gresha. We traveled in what I can only refer to as the "cattle car." The rooms, if that is what you can call them, consisted of four bunks which were too short for the average person to stretch out on. The compartment was not enclosed, but rather open to the hallway with two seats along the opposite wall. The railcar was crowded, hot, humid, and filled with a variety of smells, the most pungent odor being that of un-bathed bodies. Figuring that this was how the majority of people in Russia traveled, I layed down on my bunk and fell asleep with my clothes on. When we arrived in Visakogorny, Lydia insisted on feeding me, so it was off to her apartment before traveling on to Siziman Bay. I was relieved that this time we only had Maxim Instant Coffee and tea rather than the usual vodka.

At 2:00 a.m. we loaded up our things onto the crew bus and headed off to camp. Considering that we were still experiencing spring break-up, the season when snow melts and the ground thaws turning everything into mud, the road was in better condition than I expected it to be. The Chichimara River was running extremely high and fast. The new bridge was holding up well, but the approach was under about two feet of flowing water. We made it into camp around 7:30 a.m. Sveta immediately ran out of the office to greet me, giving me a big hug and kiss on the cheek. She had such a sweet, bubbly personality and was an absolute joy to have around. It was too bad that the Russian managers treated her so poorly. I honestly believed this was because she was not from Visakogorny or Komsomolsk. However, I considered her to be one of their most dedicated and productive employees.

Later, while having coffee with Hubert, Greg, Joe, and Misha up in the Gulag, Potarov came in to say hello. He looked pretty good, but considering his condition, I was still very surprised to see him back at camp. He greeted me with his usual enthusiastic smile and bear hug, then sat down to have some tea and BS with us. I told him about what I had been doing while in the States, and he and the others filled me in on what had happened in Siziman during my absence.

After lunch, I took a short nap then walked down to the log yard to find Big Red. Although the ice had left Siziman Bay by early April, heavy ice flows coming out of the northern Tartarskiy Strait delayed authorization of shipping operations to destinations north of Vanino until early May. Subsequently, our first vessel of the season, the *M/V Bulunkan* was scheduled to arrive on May 10th. I jokingly argued with Natasha on who owed who the case of champagne, but had already decided that I'd buy her some anyway.

M/V Bulunkan

The *M/V Bulunkan*, with its distinctive blue-green hull and white cabin, arrived at Siziman a day early, coming into dock at around 11:00 o'clock in the morning on the ninth. Up until the arrival of this vessel, we always had to take the C-Dory out into the bay and take depth measurements before any captain would come to berth. On this, his first voyage to Siziman Bay, the captain just passed this off as a waste of time and rushed right into the dock. Once the vessel was tied up to the dock, I took Sveta on board to meet the captain and get the necessary documents signed. Loading started shortly after lunch, but not until a half dozen used cars and miscellaneous appliances were unloaded. From what I understood, the crew members on vessels such as this one often have difficulty in getting paid. Subsequently, it was a common practice for them to purchase used automobiles, motorcycles, parts, appliances, etc. in Japan and bring them back to sell in Russia.

In general, the captains of these vessels really liked to talk with Americans, and this one was no different. Ivan, the jovial, fun-loving captain of this vessel, invited Joe and me up to his cabin to visit and immediately brought out a couple of bottles of vodka and some snacks from the galley. We spent the next couple of hours sitting in his master quarters just bullshitting and admiring his female companion. During our discussions, Ivan expressed concern about the depth of water alongside the dock and thought we might not be able to load to full capacity. However, on our leaving the ship, he assured us that he would load as much volume as safely possible.

Joe and I had been invited to come back to the ship for dinner at 7:00 p.m. that evening. Even though Ivan spoke fairly good English, we took Misha along to help with any necessary translations. As we climbed on board, Misha commented that "I really like this part of my job." I presented Ivan with a bottle of Crown Royal whiskey, for which he was very appreciative. The food was excellent, probably the best meal I had ever had at camp, and there was plenty of it. We ran out of vodka, but Ivan had plenty of Japanese beer and whiskey to keep us going. In addition, Ivan offered to have us try some of his private stock of flavored vodka. One bottle contained small pieces of branches from a bush common in the area and had a cinnamon-like flavor to it. The other, almost the consistency of a liqueur, contained small chunks of deer antler and surprisingly tasted quite good. After being informed of the deer antlers' effect on a man's stamina, I told Ivan, "Just what I need in a remote camp, to walk around the rest of the night with a stiff third leg and nowhere to go!"

Other than vodka and champagne, good alcohol was relatively difficult to get into camp on a regular basis. As we stood up to leave, I asked Ivan if, on his next trip back from Japan, he could bring me "a case of beer, a case of wine, and a case of whiskey," and then I jokingly added, "and a case of women." We all laughed as he answered, "*Neyht problem.*" Ivan accompanied us out on deck and, while slapping each other on the back, said good night. Joe and I had considerable difficulty walking down the ship's plank to get back onto the dock. Misha was not much help either. Even though it was late, we decided to walk back to the Gulag and hopefully sober up enough to be able to get some sleep.

Although the loading was going slower than last year, it proceeded with no significant incidents or issues to deal with. Unfortunately, this changed about 4:30 a.m. on the twelfth when loading was discontinued until noon in order to finish on an incoming tide. Ivan felt this was necessary to assure that there would be an adequate depth of water under the ship when fully loaded. During this downtime, Uyri sent two of the "American" log trucks up into the woods. Of course, due to spring break-up and poor road conditions, they got stuck and didn't return back to camp on time, causing further delay of the ship loading operations.

Once loading was finally completed, I accompanied Lena to the vessel to bring documents for the captain's signature. With the logs stacked high on deck, we were forced to walk on the outside rail of the ship, which was only about four inches wide, to get to a location where we could get on board. Lena was so scared, she was shaking, so holding on to logs as we went, I had to hold on to her as well. I thought for sure I was going to take a swim. It was even more difficult to get her to do the same getting off the vessel. The *Bulunkan* finally departed Siziman Bay at 6:00 p.m. Joe and I watched from the jetty as the vessel backed away and turned south. Joe quietly mumbled, "Now there goes a real ship from hell." I laughed as I agreed, saying, "You got that right," and the nickname forever stuck. We also had what turned out to be the beginning of a very crazy friendship between Ivan, Joe, and myself. I returned to the Gulag to rest, but not before getting Uyri to agree on keeping the American trucks out of the woods until road conditions improved.

Uyri came into the Gulag first thing the next morning and asked, "Could you do me a favor and authorize sending the American trucks out to the logging area?" "Not yet," I replied, "but I'll go check out the road conditions myself later this morning and will let you know." Uyri quickly answered that "you don't need to go to the woods; we can wait for another day." I had wanted to go check out the logging operations anyway and decided to do so after Uyri left and I finished my coffee.

Approaching the harvest area, I mumbled, "son-of-a-bitch," as I swerved to miss the Freightliner loaded with logs as it slid around a curve in the road. I got out of the pickup and climbed up onto the cab of the truck. Even though I didn't have a translator with me, my anger was sufficient to enable the driver to understand he was not to bring the truck back out. When I got to the landing, the *Kenworth* was there and in the process of being loaded. This driver soon understood that he also was not to come back out. As I walked back to the pickup through shin-high mud, I thought to myself, *No wonder Uyri was so anxious about me going to the woods, the son-of-a-bitch didn't want me to see he had already sent the two trucks out against my direction.* Since the trucks were parked by the shop when I returned to camp, I decided not to press the issue any further with Uyri. Knowing that he would spend the rest of the day nervous about being caught, I figured that this would be enough punishment for him.

Later in the day, I took the Honda down to the scalers' shack in the log yard. "Mylinky" Natasha wanted to learn how to drive the four-wheeler, and since operations were slow, I decided why not. On her first attempt, while still in reverse, she gave it full throttle, and before I could get her hand off the gas, we slammed into a light pole. Fortunately, the damage was nothing major and limited to only a small dent in the rack. Recovering from this jolt, I put the Honda in first gear and motioned for her to go again. She immediately gave the machine too much throttle, too quickly, and I almost fell off the back with her in tow. I was finally able to get her to understand that she did not need to turn the throttle all the way in order for the machine to move. Once this concept was clear, I let her drive back and forth from the sort yard to the Gulag a couple of times. The kid was nuts—she just laughed and laughed the entire time she was on the machine. I, on the other hand, didn't think I was going to survive as we zipped up and down the road.

Back at my office, I remained frustrated with how slow it seemed to be taking to load vessels. When I discussed this with Sharkoff or Potarov, they would always comment that their loading rate was comparable to Vanino's standards. I thought back to last November's storm, remembering what the Russians could do when placed under pressure. Then after reviewing the status of our log inventory, anticipated production rates, customer requests, and available vessels, I decided to take a gamble with the shipping schedule. No one else was in the building at the time, so I took the opportunity to telephone our sales representative in Japan without being overheard. We discussed the situation, and I told him to charter three vessels for immediate arrival.

Later that day, after three fax copies of signed fixture notices were received, the Russian managers went a little ballistic on me. I was sitting in the Gulag kitchen lounge having a cup of coffee when Potarov and Sharkoff rushed in, fixture notices in hand. Both men were quite vociferous in expressing their objection to this, complaining and asking, "How could Shasta be so stupid to do such a thing." Sharkoff told me that I had to "telephone the Japan office and have two of the vessels canceled."

When I told them that the vessels were chartered at my direction, Genady became unable to translate as both men began to angrily shout out at me. However, I had heard enough Russian obscenity to understand the gist of their conversations. After a few moments, I calmly informed them that we could not cancel the fixture notices without penalty and that "you both know this." I then said, "It is not my problem to figure out how you load these vessels quickly. But you do know that the Komsomolsk office will consider it your problem if we get charged with extra demurrage for keeping any vessel waiting." With that being said, the two of them turned, stormed out of the Gulag, and rushed down to the office building.

Jeff Newton made it into camp about 5:30 a.m. the morning of the fourteenth. Before his departure from the States, I had told him about the good weather we were having. He was now jokingly giving me a ration of shit about this as we looked out the window to see huge snowflakes falling to the ground. It kept snowing most of the morning, but what had accumulated on the ground by noon had melted away by evening.

Early the next day, I learned that the *M/V Sibirskiy 2115*, *M/V Sibirskiy 2119*, and *M/V Dmitriev* were racing up the Tartarskiy Strait. Apparently all three captains had quickly cleared Customs and Immigrations in Vanino and each was attempting to have his vessel arrive at Siziman Bay first in line for loading. Throughout the day, with their ETAs changing every two hours, we couldn't determine which vessel to prepare for, so we didn't. Joe had heard that it would be the *Dmitriev*, while according to Potarov's information, the *2115* was in the lead. Before heading off to bed that night, I bet the both of them a bottle of vodka it would be the *2119*, although by both accounts, this vessel was behind the other two.

On the morning of the sixteenth, I awoke early and was down on the jetty by 5:30 a.m., just in time to see a ship coming up the Strait. Within an hour, Joe, Greg, and I were trying to follow directions from the crew in order to tie the *M/V Sibirskiy 2119* up to the dock.

No one else from camp was around, so the three of us were on our own. With increased frustration, the crew members were frantically shouting out their instructions to us. I looked up at one of them and replied, "*Amerikanski; neyht-pahneemaht,*" which means, "American; I don't understand." The expression on his face was like, oh Lord, and then with the use of more hand gestures, he continued to guide us through the docking procedure. Thirty minutes later, with still no Russians from camp in sight, we managed to secure the vessel. Once I was able to relax, I slapped Joe on his shoulder and said, "Looks like I'm two bottles of vodka richer!" "Well, you owe me a bottle," he immediately replied. "I'm too old for this type of shit." "Yeah," I said, "I haven't worked up that much sweat in such a short time since the last time I had sex. Later tonight we can empty a bottle together." "I'll agree with that," he replied. We stood waiting for the gang plank to be lowered, and I looked out into the bay to see the *M/V Dmitriev* setting anchor.

The *Sibirskiy*, with its rusty gray hull, was a different class of vessel than that of the *Bulunkan*. With a considerably less draft requirement, this "river-ocean" class vessel has the ability to travel up rivers such as the Amur, whereas the *Bulunkan* was limited to coastal travel. Coming into berth, the *Sibirskiy* bobbed like a cork on the water, swaying to and fro with each passing swell. The smaller *Dmitriev*, also a river-ocean class vessel, had two cranes situated on its deck to facilitate loading if necessary. "Damn, these vessels are great," I commented to Joe. "I sure wish I could use one of them to harvest all that white spruce dying up the Kuskokwim River in Alaska." "Ah hell," he grumbled, "even if you could use 'em, the greenies would stop you from logging over there anyway." "Yeah, I suppose you're right," I replied, "but they sure would do the job."

The *Sibirskiy 2119* left the dock around 4 o'clock in the morning on the eighteenth, loaded with a record 4,250 cubic meters of logs. The *Dmitriev* tied up at 7:00 a.m., and when the fog lifted a couple of hours later, the *M/V Sibirskiy 2115* could be seen anchored in the bay. The Russian managers were going nuts, but I loved it. Apparently the managers back in the Komsomolsk office wanted to slow down the loading time. I believe this was primarily because they did not understand the new shipping contract negotiated for the year and its advantages over the previous year's. However, as long as I could keep bringing ships into Siziman Bay "back-to-back" like this, they couldn't buck me, and I had vessels scheduled to arrive every two to three days through the entire month of June.

I guess I had been in Russia too long. While I was watching the ship-loading operations, the captain of the *Dmitriev* saw me walking around on deck and said, "*Dohbra ohtra*" (Good morning). I answered, "*Dohbra ohtra.*" He nodded his head and replied, "*Khak de la?*" (How are you?), to which I responded, "*Normalna*" (Normal). Apparently thinking that I was one of the Russian managers, he continued to converse with me, in Russian of course. I had to quickly interrupt him telling him, "*Eezveenyehteh, Amerikanski neyht panymayht,*" which is "Excuse me; American; I don't understand." Then to my surprise, he began to speak fluent English.

Not too long after lunch, Potarov and Genady came into my office. Closing the door, Genady said, "Nikolay would like to talk with you if you have the time." "No problem," I replied. "What's up?" With Genady translating, Potarov explained, "As you know, I have a problem with my heart." Pausing briefly to let out a deep breath, he then continued, "I've recently been to Moscow and have consulted with several doctors there. The operation that I need can be performed in Russia, but it is not common." "What type of operation do you need?" I asked. He quietly replied, "A triple bypass," adding that "I was told it is common and very successful in the United States." Genady commented that "this type of surgery performed in Russia has less than a 50 percent chance of recovery." I leaned forward in my chair and asked, "Nikolay, what is it that I can do to help?" I could see his eyes watering up as he requested if I could "talk with the people in Philadelphia and ask if Frontier would help to bring me to America for this surgery." "Nikolay, of course I will talk with them. You are a good friend and a valuable asset to this operation," I added, "I'll see what I can do." Potarov leaned forward, placed his hand on my knee, and in English said, "Thank you," then quietly left. I knew that Nikolay carried a bottle of nitroglycerin with him at all times. Although he didn't come right out and say it, I think that his life expectancy without the operation was short.

M/V Dmitriev, M/V Sibirskiy 2115 and
M/V Shchetinin

The *M/V Shchetinin*, Russian for "bristle face," arrived the next morning and set anchor about 5:30 a.m. It looked like a scene out of an old World War II movie with three rusty old ships out in the bay, sitting ducks for a bombing raid or submarine attack.

Loading of the *Dmitriev* finished around 9 o'clock in the evening, exceeding our previous loading rates by one and a half times. In doing so, the Siziman Bay operation established a new standard for which other ports on the east coast of Russia were evaluated on. Shortly after midnight, with 3,310 cubic meters of logs on board, the vessel departed. What started earlier in the evening as a light drizzle had now turned into a significant rainstorm that would put the Pacific Northwest to shame.

The *M/V Sibirskiy 2115* came to berth and was secured to the dock around 4:00 a.m. on the twentieth. Within three and a half hours, loading operations had begun. The rain that had continued for most of the night had stopped, but there was a heavy *tumaan* (fog) which remained, covering the shoreline all day. The fog was so thick, we were unable to see the *Shchetinin* anchored out in the bay until it was early evening.

Andrei came into camp in the afternoon and had me up to his room to catch up on operations and bullshit. Normally we would not talk about politics, but I was curious what he thought about the upcoming presidential election in June. He was surprisingly open with me on the subject, commenting that he didn't expect much to change in Russia. "The current government officials [Yeltsin] were previously communists." Adding that "the only difference between them and the present-day communist party is that the old communists have already stolen money from the system, and the new communists now want their turn to steal."

Later that evening I learned that Olga, one of the scalers, had been fired last week, which explained why I hadn't seen her around camp this shift. From what Misha understood, apparently the wife of some guy in camp that Olga was "sleeping with" complained to the Komsomolsk office and asked them to do something about it. So, true to Russian tradition, they kept the asshole and let a good worker go. Frustrating, this place was so ridiculously petty at times. Greg took the news kind of hard. He and Olga were starting to get fairly close, so this really got him down.

The Russians had been busy all day cleaning up the camp and preparing for the arrival of the "Commission" on the twenty-second. Apparently there was a large group of people to be descending upon us, half of which were various government officials. Along with some individuals from Komsomolsk, including that drunken son-of-a-bitch, Nazarkin, a few folks from the Philadelphia office were coming in as well. This unfortunately this included our favorite idiot, John Cardinal. Since my prayers didn't seem to be answered lately, I got the Russians in camp praying for fog so that the helicopter wouldn't be able to fly.

Unfortunately there was no fog, so the helicopter arrived in camp mid-afternoon as scheduled with our guests—twenty in all. Once people were shown to their rooms and given a chance to freshen up, the grand tour of the camp facilities, log yard, and jetty was given. The first stop was always the well which was the source of water for the camp. People were always impressed by the quality of this water as compared to the rusty, foul tasting liquid found in city water systems. Most had never drank water directly from the tap before without having to boil it first. Following the tour, we had a very nice dinner but without the usual "toasts" given out. This was very strange, and I was not sure if it meant that the previous day's discussions did not go well in Komsomolsk, or what.

Later that evening, Svetlana, an attorney for the Philadelphia office and a native Russian from Moscow, commented to me that she was impressed by how the Russians sought me out on their arrival and greeted me with general appreciation and affection. She explained that she hadn't observed this toward any other American involved with the Siziman Bay project. We sat for a while in the Gulag kitchen, relaxing with some coffee over casual conversation. Svetlana was an intelligent, confident young woman, and I complimented her on her expertise and negotiating skills "at the table." However, all the while I was thinking how nice it would have been to see her tall, shapely body lying naked on my bed. After all, she, like most other Russian women, was extremely attractive which made it difficult for me to concentrate on anything else.

In the morning, I was able to sneak Bailey and Cardinal out of camp and up to the harvest areas to show them what was really going on out there. We stopped, and I showed them Tonguska Creek which was flowing a muddy brown from heavy siltation due to the logging further on up the valley. When we arrived at the landing area, both were amazed to see streams of silt-laden water flowing down the skid trails and onto the landing, turning the area into a slimy mud bog. "This operation is the worst environmental degradation that I've ever been involved in," I commented. Just then, one of the rubber-tired skidders came down the creek bed of a small tributary to Tonguska Creek, dropped its load of tree-length logs on the landing, and disappeared back up the creek.

Government Inspection of Operations

Appalled at what he just observed, Bailey asked, "Can't you do anything about this?" "George," I answered, "believe it or not, it is actually getting better, but under the current organization, I have very little control over the woods operations. I've been able to force my authority over what happens in the sort yard and on ship-loading operations. But, this was only because I realized early on that that was where I could initially make the biggest impact on the profitability of the operation. Most of the crew respect me, and to the extent they can work with me on operational issues they do, but the bottom line is that I am not the person they report to." "Jesus, we certainly can't let the OPIC boys see this," he replied, adding, "I can see the urgency in having you formally designated as vice president of Dalny-Les so we can put an end to this question of your authority here. We'll be sure to address this issue with Nazarkin once we get back to Komsomolsk." After returning back to camp, we joined the group and headed down to the beach for a picnic-style (*shaslik*) lunch.

Bailey was in my office when I got a call from our sales representative in the Tokyo office. The customer in Japan was threatening to submit a claim against Dalny-Les on quality issues for logs recently shipped. He and Osika Corporation wanted me to go to Japan from the thirty-first to the fifth to discuss and hopefully resolve a number of issues and their concerns. If it were up to that idiot Cardinal, I wouldn't go, but Bailey overrode him and instructed me to do it. I was to leave camp on Sunday, meet with them in Komsomolsk on Monday, arrive in Khabarovsk on Tuesday morning, and fly to Japan on Wednesday. With that decided, they boarded the helicopter with the rest of the group and departed. "Joe," I said as we watched the helicopter disappear over the hill, "I need a drink." "Let's go, buddy," he replied, "always happy to help you out."

Loading of the *Schetinin* was completed around 6:30 a.m. the morning of the twenty-fourth. After Lena had the captain sign all the necessary documents, we stayed to chat and have some tea. With 3,425 cubic meters of sawlogs on board, the captain wanted to wait for the high tide at one o'clock in the afternoon before leaving the bay. The ship had a problem with one of its ballast pumps and was listing to one side quite a bit—enough so that you had to lean in the opposite direction order to stand up. For the remainder of the day, most of the people in camp were worthless as far as work was concerned, taking a well-deserved breather.

The *Captain Moranseff*, a small landing craft, arrived the next morning with three small prefab housing units. I was both surprised and irritated that the container of supplies and spare parts from the United States was not on board. We had been waiting for this since February and had been told it had cleared customs, so other than for pure stupidity, there was no reason for the container not to have been sent in first.

While down in the log yard, Big Red openly defied my directions by telling me, in front of the other scalers, that she "would not load 8.1 meter logs on the next ship until instructed to by Potarov or Sharkoff." This was very unusual for her to act this way, and I was not in the mood to put up with it. "Natasha," I angrily answered back, "if those logs do not get loaded on the vessel because of you, then this shift will be the last for you at Siziman Bay. I will discuss the issue with Phillipov and have you fired." As I walked away, I told Genady, "I really hate having to make this type of threat in order to get things done." "No, it was a good thing for you to do this," he replied. "You have treated her and the other crew members too good for so long that they have forgotten that you are also the boss." I thought to myself this might be true, but I still felt miserable after one of these confrontations but I guess it's the Russian way.

Even though I'd been getting up to twelve hours of sleep the previous two nights, I still had to take a nap by noon. The day before, I slept for four hours, and this morning, I laid down at 10:30 a.m. and didn't wake up for three hours. For some reason, I just didn't seem to have much energy.

I left camp on the morning of the twenty-sixth, arriving in Visakogorny before noon. Potarov took me out to his dacha, a small garden plot with a shack that reminded me of one of my "camps" I built as a kid. The short trip reconfirmed in my mind what a dump this town really was. I found it hard to believe that people could have any happiness living under conditions like I saw in this village. I caught the noon train and arrived in Komsomolsk at 7:00

p.m., sleeping most of the trip. A driver for Dalny-Les met me at the station and dropped me off on the street near the apartment. Fortunately, Sam Carlson was at home to let me in, since I did not have a key.

After dropping my bags off, I ventured out to a small grocery store nearby to buy some food. My Russian was improving, but I still had some minor communication problems with the clerk. However, I only ended up with one extra item that I didn't really want, but it was easier to purchase it than it was to try and explain for her to take it back. Back at the apartment, Sam told me, "It's official, they made you vice president." Cardinal came back to the apartment about 9:00 p.m. totally shit-faced drunk from spending the day with Phillipov. I didn't really want to, but I took him for a two-and-a-half-hour walk down by the Amur River and through a couple of parks so he could sober up a little before going to bed. I figured if I hadn't taken him out, it would have been puke city for him, and I didn't want to have to listen to that all night. It was difficult for me to have any respect or much use for the man.

The trained pulled into Khabarovsk at 6:45 a.m. on the twenty-eighth, and surprisingly enough, I was met by a Dalny Resources driver. This was the first time in the four trips I had made to Khabarovsk that someone from the company had met me at the station. I guess being Vice President had at least some perks to it. The cabin on the train was quite hot, and I hadn't been able to sleep very well, so after checking into the Parus Hotel, I slept for a couple of hours before going to the Shasta office.

Joe called to give me an update on what was happening at Siziman Bay. "The *Gorbachevskiy* had one hold loaded by seven o'clock this morning, and we should finish another by around five-thirty this evening. The *Bulunkan* just set anchor out in the bay, and we still haven't heard what to load or where it's going to." I told him, "I'll check on this today and will let you know later." Joe then informed me that "Newton tore some muscles in his shoulder while working on one of the Timbcos. He's lost all mobility of his right arm, and I've got him in a sling." About all I could say was, "Damn, sounds bad!" "I think so," Joe replied. "He's going to be leaving camp on Wednesday with Taylor and Hubert to catch the Alaska Airlines flight on Friday back to the States for treatment."

After lunch, Olga went with me to the travel agency at the Intourist Hotel to help purchase my tickets for Japan. To get to Tokyo, I had to fly to Amori on Hokkaido and then transfer to a shuttle airline from there. Olga laughed when I told her, "I hope that someone there speaks English, or I might end up on a plane to Singapore!" As we walked back to the office, Olga asked, "When are you going to start working for Shasta?" "What makes you think I'm going to do that?" I replied. "Oh, just intuition," she said, smiling shyly.

I walked on, quietly thinking about the difficultly I was having with making a decision regarding this. Career wise, it was probably a better opportunity for me than with Frontier. Living in Khabarovsk in my own apartment would certainly be more comfortable than my little cubbyhole in the Gulag at Siziman Bay. God only knows why, but I had this underlying sense of loyalty to the Siziman Bay project. Everyone said that I had made a significant change in the viability of the operation, although I tended to think they overemphasized my contribution. The Russians seemed to truly like me, and most of the expats had told me that if I were to ever leave, they would follow right after—which I guess is a compliment of sorts. "Olga," I finally said, "if it meant that I would be able to look at your beautiful self every day, I just might have to do it!" Blushing, Olga replied, "Oh, Pol," and giggling turned her head away.

I had asked Olga out for a date before, but because Shasta was under contract with Frontier she considered it against company policy. Joe told me that in March he had stopped by the Shasta office to say hello and happened to meet with one of Olga's girlfriends. According to him, this young woman was a very pleasant and beautiful, blue-eyed, brunette. In his continued attempt to find me female companionship, Joe had asked this girl if she'd be interested in going out on a blind-date with me. She was, but apparently Olga abruptly intervened saying "No, she cannot go out with Paul." When Joe asked her why not, Olga replied that if she couldn't go out with me then neither could any of her girlfriends. Such is the mind of Russian women.

When staying at the Parus Hotel, you never knew who you might meet. I had breakfast with a man from Yellowknife, Northwest Territories, and a woman from Calgary, Alberta. They apparently were going to spend a month somewhere south of Khabarovsk as missionaries, trying to bring Christianity into a country of what I considered a relatively religious people already. I felt their attitude toward the Russians rather condescending and thought it would have been better for them to have brought vodka and champagne instead of the hundred-plus eyeglasses donated by their churches.

I caught the afternoon Aeroflot flight on the twenty-ninth to Amori, Japan. The Immigrations Officer in Khabarovsk questioned my ability to fly to Japan without a special visa. However, after a few minutes, I was finally able to convince her that, unlike Russians, Americans really could travel freely to Japan. I don't know if she truly understood my broken Russian or if she just got tired of listening to me. Sitting in the lobby waiting to board the airplane, I noticed that I was the only non-Asian on the flight. We arrived in Amori on time, and while passing through security, I set off the alarm system. They didn't have a bowl for me to empty my pockets into, so a guard took the wand to me. I was not too concerned when she reached into my front pocket and grabbed my knife, but was taken by surprise when reaching for my belt buckle, her hand slid down inside my pants. Cleared, we both smiled at each other, and I passed on through.

I was supposed to call Takahara after purchasing my ticket to Tokyo; however, there was nowhere to exchange my Russian rubles or US dollars for Japanese yen at the airport. I didn't have the proper coins to use the public telephones, so I went back to the JAS ticket counter to see if anyone could help me out. The Airline Agent I had purchased my ticket from knew very little English and was so cute while trying to help me. After a few minutes of using a combination of sign language, picture drawings, and short-worded sentences, she was finally able to understand my problem. She telephoned Takahara for me, and I was able to inform him of my arrival time into Tokyo.

Having a little time before my flight, I walked around the airport looking at the photos and exhibits showcasing the island of Hokkaido. I noticed that once again I appeared to be the only Caucasian in the place. The flight to the Tokyo Haneda Corporation Airport was relatively short. While the airport in Amori was calm and relaxing, the pace inside this huge terminal was hectic. After a number of attempts, I found a younger Japanese girl who spoke English, and I was able to get directions to where I would find Takahara waiting for me. Other than appearing to be the only white boy in the place, the thing that impressed me about the Amori and Haneda airports was the absolute cleanliness of both terminals.

Once I met up with Takahara, we took the train to the Akasaka district where I'd be staying at the Capitol Tokyu Hotel (very nice). After a quick shave and shower, we walked down a narrow alley lined by restaurants, small shops, and nightclubs. Takahara's restaurant of choice for the night was located in the basement of one of the buildings, and although small, the food was excellent and apparently known locally for its wine selection. I finally got to bed at 11:30 p.m., which with the two-hour time difference, meant it was more like 1:30 a.m. to my system. I didn't think to close the window curtains, and by 4:30 in the morning, daylight was filling my room making it difficult to sleep until 6:00 a.m. as I had wanted to.

Takahara came by the hotel at seven o'clock in the morning., and we took a taxi to the train station to catch the 8:05 a.m. *shinkansen* (bullet train) for a two-hour ride to Onahama. I was told that these electric trains could reach speeds of up to 210 kilometers per hour, although the fastest on this trip was 160 kilometers per hour. With seats much like those in an airplane, the ride was smooth and extremely comfortable. We were met outside the station in Onahama by Osika Corporation's customer and taken to the port area. The customer informed me that 10 percent of the logs being imported through this port were coming from Siziman Bay. After spending a couple of hours looking at logs from Siziman Bay and discussing quality issues, we went to a small sushi restaurant for lunch. Takahara and I were back on the shinkansen to Tokyo at 1:30 p.m. and exhausted; we both slept most of the trip. Once back in Tokyo, we transferred to the 4:10 p.m. shinkansen for Gamagori.

I kept close to Takahara as we hurried from one station platform to the other. The Tokyo Station is a constant mass of Japanese rushing about in every direction. I feared that if I lost sight of Takahara, I would be lost in the station forever. Traveling south of Tokyo, the area becomes more mountainous than north toward Onahama. Along the way, I was able to catch a glimpse of Mt. Fuji, partially hidden by the clouds. Like Mt. Rainier in Washington State, this mountain was also an impressive-looking volcano, rising high above everything around it. We transferred to a local train in Toyashi and after a short fifteen-minute ride, arrived in Gamagori around seven in the evening. Takahara and I were taken directly to Osika's office to meet Kikuma and ended up negotiating a cargo line-up for another shipment.

I telephoned Joe Dill at Siziman Bay, and he excitedly exclaimed, "Where the hell are you? The *Bulunkan* is coming into the dock right now, and we haven't heard anything from James on what to load or where it's supposed to go to!" "Joe," I calmly replied, "Load it for Gamagori. I'll fax you the cargo plan in a couple of minutes." "Will do," he answered. "How's Japan?" "The food is good, and so is the beer, wine, and sake," I added. "I'm beginning to think I need to send at least one messed up shipload of logs a month so I can come over here and enjoy." "You pot licker," Joe growled. "You get your ass back over here quick, and don't forget the booze." I hung up, told Takahara and Kikuma, "We'll start loading the *Bulunkan* tonight for Gamagori." Once I faxed the cargo plan to Siziman Bay, we left the office for dinner which included an excellent variety of sushi, tempura, fried fish, and vegetables. The woman who owned the restaurant knew Kikuma and was quite interested in learning about this crazy American living in Russia. During our conversation, I learned that the dishes we were using were over 150 years old.

I settled into my room at the Higaki Hotel around 11:00 p.m. A traditional Japanese-style hotel which involved sleeping on the floor, it also included a hot springs spa which I took advantage of before going to sleep. Not having a swim suit and not knowing if I was even supposed to, I was fortunate to have the entire area to myself as I swam bare-ass naked around the pool. Breakfast in the morning consisted of clam soup, fish, and tofu. I could do without seafood that early in the day, so I was happy to see there was also a small lettuce salad with tomato and slice of ham for me to eat.

We spent the better part of the morning at the port, inspecting logs recently delivered on the *Sibirskiy 2115*. "Takahara-san," I said, "I don't know what happened with the sorting for the 3.8 meter logs, but I agree with you, many of these logs look like pulp! Please assure your customer that I will take care of this once I get back to Siziman Bay." The 8.1 meter and 7.6 meter logs, however, "look real good," I argued, "and I will not accept any quality claim on these sorts." The market conditions in Japan had become real tight, and customers were becoming increasingly picky—which by the way, the Japanese are very good at. Although this customer had a valid issue with the quality of the 3.8 meter sort, I think he threw in a complaint on the longer logs just for testing this new supplier.

Takahara and I caught the 1:20 p.m. train back to Tokyo and the Osika office. Our meeting ended around 8:00 p.m., and I was taken to a very nice upscale sushi bar atop one of the taller office buildings in the area. The view overlooking the lights of Tokyo was incredible as was the food. The exception to this was the one piece of salmon sashimi in which I found a worm. Not wanting to embarrass my gracious hosts, I quickly removed the curled-up little critter with my chopsticks and dropped it to the floor under the table. Then, after eating the tasty piece of raw meat, offered a toast so that I could kill off any ill-effects with a good shot of sake.

Takahara came by the hotel early in the morning on June 1st to escort me through the Tokyo Station one last time. Without him, there was no way I could have found my way to the correct shinkansen bound for Niigata. The two-and-a-half-hour Aeroflot flight from Niigata to Khabarovsk was uneventful, and after checking in at the Parus, I decided to wander around town. The weather was pleasantly warm, and I ended up down by the Amur River listening to music being play by some DJ in the park and watching people dance. The young women's skirts were, as usual, short, and their high heel shoes accentuated the curves of their toned, model-quality legs. Admiring their style, I thought, *Why in the hell can't the women back in the States be like this?* A brief thundershower passed through, soaking everyone who was caught outside. While walking back to the hotel, my attention and direction of travel were diverted to a gorgeous young blonde wearing a short white dress. As with everyone else, she was drenched to the bone. The features of her slender body had become clearly visible underneath the wet fabric clinging to her skin, accentuated only by the white bra and thong panties she wore. It was like having my own wet T-shirt contest ten feet away as she walked up the boulevard, seemingly without a care.

After changing into some dry clothes, I stopped at the Shasta office to telephone Joe at Siziman Bay. When he answered and learned it was me, he blurted out, "Where the hell are you now, and when are you getting your butt back here?" "Joe," I answered, "you sound beat. What's up?" He replied, "You really need to be careful what you request from these captains, especially Ivan. He brought back your cases of beer, wine, and whiskey this trip." "All right," I said excitedly. "So what's wrong with that? You old fart, you didn't drink it all did you?" "No I didn't, you pot licker," he replied. "Ivan had enough booze for everyone, but do you remember what else you asked for?" I thought for a second, but before I could answer, Joe blurted out, "*Women* you stupid Boy Scout; you asked for a case of women! Well, the crazy bastard stopped by Nakhodka on the way back and brought ten women with him!"

Such was my first lesson in being careful of what you happen to ask a Russian for. Apparently there were bonfires and *shashlik* (shishkabob) on the beach every night, food and drinks on board the vessel, and an occasional visit to the banya involved. "It was almost one continuous party from the time they started loading logs until the documents were signed and the ship left." I figured it was best not to ask for any more details, but understood that this particular visit of the *Bulunkan* would be remembered by some for quite a long time.

Later I had a few drinks in the bar at the Parus, mainly talking with the bartender, Zhenya. As with the other hotel employees, Zhenya knew me fairly well by now, and he was always willing to keep me company. A guy from California walked in, and upon hearing us speaking English, immediately sat down next to me. Kurt was in Khabarovsk for his first time, so I gave him a quick overview of the city and the Russian Far East in general.

As usual, the conversation turned to the Russian women. "The women here are beautiful," he exclaimed. "I agree; they're amazing," I replied, adding that "I believe they are the real reason for the Cold War between the United States and Russia." Kurt shot me a puzzled look. "Think about it," I continued. "Obviously the men in Russia knew what a good thing they had over here and wanted their government to keep it a secret. On the other hand, our government was so afraid of spies, that they kept it a secret as well. Do you think that if the American men knew how beautiful the Russian women were that we would have stood still and let our government keep the

Cold War going as long as it did?" Kurt chuckled as he took a sip of his beer and answered, "You're probably right." I continued, "You know the saying Keep America Beautiful? Well, if we really wanted to beautify America, we should make it easier for Russian women to immigrate into the States!" We clinked our bottles together and noticing a big smile on Zhenya's face, told him how lucky he was.

Kurt was interested in checking out other bars, so after finishing our beers, we took the short walk down to the Intourist Hotel. Being the major hotel in Khabarovsk, the Intourist had a choice of Russian, European, Korean, and Japanese restaurants to choose from. In addition, there was a "pool" bar in the basement floor and a "club" bar on the eleventh floor. We decided to check out the bar upstairs, and to my surprise, they had live entertainment that evening. The singer, backed up by a karaoke machine and saxophone player, actually sounded fairly decent. The three long-legged, scantily clad, Las Vegas—style dancers on stage with him would have kept our interest no matter what music was playing. However, when six young dancers wearing red two-piece bikinis, panty hose, and high heels came out on the floor, we couldn't handle it and left, totally disgusted. When I say "young," considering their lack of physical development, I guessed these girls could not have been any older than twelve to fourteen years.

The Summer of '96

I caught the ten o'clock train the next evening, and at 6:30 a.m. on the morning of the third I arrived in Komsomolsk. I was not too surprised that upon exiting the terminal out into the parking area, there was no one from Dalny-Les to meet me. I caught a taxi, and with some difficulty in communication, eventually made it to the office. I had a slight problem in getting the security guard to give me the key to the "Americans" office. After a few minutes of frustration, I not-so-calmly said, "I am Vice President of Dalny-Les" and with outstretched hand, shouted, "Now give me the fucking key!" I'm not sure if he really understood my English or not, but he certainly understood the anger in my voice. He reluctantly handed me the key, but only after I signed his checkout sheet. I don't know what the hell they thought I would want to steal from this place, but I would go through this hassle every time I came to Komsomolsk. You would think they could remember me. Fortunately, I was able to wash my hair and shave in the bathroom sink before everyone else began to arrive around 9:00 a.m.

Nadia, having spent time in Khabarovsk visiting her daughter and mother, arrived later in the day, and together we caught the 7:20 p.m. train to Visakogorny. I immediately went to sleep while she listened to country-western music on my Walkman. The train pulled into

Visakogorny around 2:45 a.m. the next morning, on time as usual. Potarov met us as we got off and took us to the supply truck that he had arranged to take me out to camp. I helped Nadia up into the cab and climbed in after her. A six-wheel-drive KMAZ truck is not a comfortable vehicle to ride in by any means. It was usually a miserable ride along much of the rough road back to camp. Once we were on our way, Nadia immediately tried to fall asleep. After an hour or so of watching her head snap back and forth, I felt sorry for her, as well as being concerned that she'd break her neck. I put my arm around her and told her to lean up against me and lay her head on my shoulder. For the remainder of the trip, she slept peacefully, snuggled up next to me.

This simple act of kindness turned out to be a huge mistake. Maybe under similar circumstances Russian men would not have shown the same level of compassion, I don't know, but Nadia read much more into my assistance than I had intended. Later in the day after we arrived Siziman Bay, I noticed Nadia trying to spend more time than usual being around me. She even followed me down to the beach when I went fishing that evening. Before traveling to Japan, I had noticed the Russians placing long gill nets offshore. Thinking that perhaps they were fishing for salmon, I decided to try my luck. So with spinning rod in hand, I walked about a half mile down the beach from camp and started casting out into the water just before high tide. Nadia eventually got tired of waiting around and soon left me to myself. Although I didn't catch anything, it was nice just to be alone and relax as the day ended.

Joe Dill with Kumja caught from beach

I continued trying different locations along the beach over a three-day period, for which I had only gotten chuckles from the Russians tending their nets. Finally on the evening of June 8th I landed a nice fish of about six pounds in size. The next day, Joe decided to come with me, and he landed an eight-pounder. Subsequently, "*Kumja!*" became the cry for "fish on" among the expats when hooking into this spirited fighting fish similar to the Dolly Varden found off the west coast of North America. We continued to fish the high tides for the next week, catching at least one fish each night, the largest being one about ten pounds that Joe caught.

Nadia continued to tag along with me wherever I would go. If I went to the office, she'd follow. When I'd go to the log yard, the Gulag, or wherever, it didn't matter; she would soon show up. Her attention toward me did not go without notice, and one evening Joe said, "You know buddy, Nadia obviously wants to hook up with you, and you could certainly do worse. Besides, I'm a little concerned about your loneliness." "Yeah, right," I mumbled sarcastically. Joe added, "Well maybe I'll have to have a talk with her, you know, give her some insight on your quirks." "Joe, you son of a bitch," I shouted, half laughing, "Don't you dare encourage her. You know damn well that I have no desire to get involved with any woman here in camp or in Russia for that matter." Joe laughed and said, "Well, you know you've got a problem with her. How 'bout we go have a couple of drinks to ease your pain?" "You asshole," I replied, "Let's go." With Nadia, it reached the point where the only relief I got was to jump into one of the pickup trucks and go out to the logging sites to get away.

The M/V *Sibirskiy 2119* had arrived on the ninth. The next evening while the vessel was being loaded, we expats kind of said "the hell with it all," and along with Misha and Genady, went down to the beach for a bonfire, shashlik, and vodka. We were able to catch a couple of kumja and bake them over the fire. Sveta had heard that we were going and asked if she and Galena could join us, to which we said, "Of course." A couple of the gals from the ship were already on the beach, so we invited them to join us as well.

I don't know about the others, but for me, these beach parties were a relaxing departure from the fast-paced craziness of the daily business at Siziman Bay. Work-related issues were rarely discussed, but rather it was a time for bullshitting and the bonding of friendships. We Americans would often talk about life back in the States and our impressions of Russia. The Russians would explain changes in their lives since perestroika and their hopes for the future. Usually though, the conversations were more jovial in nature while we drank vodka, listened to music, danced a little, and generally enjoyed each other's company.

When loading of the vessel was finished on the eleventh, the Russian crews had blown their previous loading rates completely "out-of-the-water." In addition, the *Sibirskiy 2119* departed with an impressive 4,787.6 cubic meters of spruce sawlogs on board, setting a new record for the amount of volume loaded on this class of vessel. I was told later that upon hearing of this, the ship owners closed up their office for the remainder of the day then went out and got drunk. Watching that vessel back away from the jetty then turning south toward Vanino, I don't think I had ever been more proud of any group of people that I've worked with than at that time. After the ship left, Joe and I went fishing, and I landed a nice kumja about eight pounds or so in size. It was a beautiful evening, the first in a week with no fog, so Joe and I stayed till after dark. The beach was real peaceful as we sat and talked about what we wanted in our lives and why in the hell we were there at Siziman Bay.

Later that night, I was in my office working late, as I often did, taking advantage of the silence that allowed me to stay focused on the business at hand. Not too long after I was there, I heard the outside door close. I was hoping it might be Misha coming down to practice his English translations on the computer, but it turned out to be Nadia. Upon entering my office, she took off her heavy coat, revealing an extremely tight-fitting sweater that accentuated her ample sized breasts. As she walked toward me, the scent of her perfume filled the room. She sat down on my desk, leaned forward, and asked, "What are you doing down here so late at night?" Leaning back in my chair, I replied, "Not much else to do, so I often come down here to be by myself, listen to music, and do some work." I knew why she was there and what she wanted to do, so I continued to work on my computer, attempting to ignore her. Nadia stood up and moved behind me, and I soon found the back of my head placed snugly between her tits as she began to rub my shoulders. I quickly turned around in my chair and gently pushed her back. "Nadia," I started, "I'm sorry if I gave you the wrong impression, but I am not interested in having a relationship with you. I'm not interested in having relationship with anyone, so you need to just stop." I felt terrible as I watched her eyes fill with tears, but I just couldn't let this continue. She turned, grabbing her coat as she went out the door—and that was that. We went from her following me around everywhere to completely avoiding me for the next couple of weeks. Things finally got back to normal when Doc returned to camp and they started banging each other again in her room. Since her room was next to mine, the sounds emanating from these frequent encounters were also a reason why I'd go to my office late at night.

June 15th brought on another crew shift change, and although little work gets accomplished on these days, I got up at 6:30 a.m. anyway. I worked in the office until about ten-thirty and feeling poorly, had to go back to bed. My shit had been charcoal black for a number of days, and Joe swore that it was due to internal bleeding in the stomach, suggesting that it was undigested blood. Since I didn't trust Doc to check me out, I figured I'd just keep an eye on it. Four hours later I woke up and headed back down to the office. Nobody was in the mood to work, so I ended up bringing Misha and Sveta back up to the Gulag for a glass of wine and casual conversation before they headed out of camp for their fifteen days off. They were interested, so I ended up showing them a video of my recent trip to Maui. Whether I took the job with Shasta or not, I had arranged for them to hire Sveta to handle all of their shipping documentation. The Russians here continued to treat her as fourth class, and she deserved a better opportunity than what Siziman Bay or Dalny-Les could provide her.

Joe, Chuck, Mike, and I took advantage of the lack of activity and went fishing in the evening. Chuck caught a real nice eight-pounder, and Joe found four Japanese glass fishing floats while beachcombing. All I did was to get caught on the wrong side of the rock point on an incoming tide. I got soaked getting back around it, but it was better than having to spend all night on the beach. I also picked up my first tick of the season, catching the little bugger just as it was starting to dig into the back of my neck.

During the winter, the inventory of *dravah* and the size of these log decks continued to increase. By the time the shipping season arrived, a considerable area within the sort yard was being taken up by these "reject" logs. I remained frustrated with the Russian managers' position that this quality of log was "unacceptable to ship." A couple of days before the *M/V Gorbachevskiy* was due to arrive for a shipment of pulpwood, I took Joe with me to once again inspect the quality of this log sort. We climbed over, walked around and in between these decks, discussing what we would have done if these logs were in Alaska. I then decided to take a risk. The morning that the vessel arrived, I told Joe we were going to mix some of the *dravah* in with the standard pulpwood.

By mid-afternoon, loading of the pulpwood had commenced as usual. However, later that night after the Russian managers had quit work for the day, I took Joe and Misha down to the log yard to meet with the crew. I instructed them that I wanted every third bundle of logs to be taken from the *dravah* log decks, and to record it as pulpwood. The crew was nervous and concerned about the consequences in doing this, expressing that it was not allowed under GOST, and the Komsomolsk office had not authorized it. However, over the previous months, I had developed enough credibility and respect from the Russian workers that they said they would do as I requested. I left Joe in the log yard to make sure that they pulled logs from the decks that I wanted, and I went down to the jetty to watch the loading operations before heading back to the Gulag for the night.

Following the arrival of the *Gorbachevskiy* to its destination in Japan, I nervously waited to hear from the customer regarding this shipment. After two weeks had passed with no word regarding any quality claim, I figured that my intuition was correct. I repeated this loading procedure of one-third *dravah* to two-thirds pulpwood during the next three pulp shipments, and not once did we receive any comments from Japan on poor or unacceptable quality. It wasn't until after the Russians prepared their monthly report on production, shipments, and inventory that their managers learned that they had shipped more pulpwood than they produced. When they finally realized that the *dravah* log decks no longer existed, they immediately put blame on the log yard crew and scalers. Misha rushed into the Gulag and told me, "Potarov and Sharkoff are really chewing ass at Natasha about shipping the *dravah*."

On hearing this, we both ran down to the office and interrupted the meeting. I explained to the both of them that I had instructed and authorized the loading of the *dravah* on the pulp shipments. They immediately started to object to my actions. I asked them, "Have you heard of any quality claim issues from including the *dravah* in with the pulpwood?" Their reply was, "No, but—" I stopped them short, saying, "I just increased the profitability of this operation, and Siziman Bay has changed the standards acceptable for pulpwood shipments to Japan. Do you really have a problem with this? Natasha and the log yard crew did exactly as I instructed. If you still have a problem with what I did, you need to contact Philadelphia." From that point on, we basically stopped generating *dravah* log decks, and our pulp shipments continued to be accepted without complaint.

I woke up early as I often did, grabbed a cup of coffee, and drove down to the beach. Unlike the usual reddish-orange hued sunrises of before, this mid-July morning sky turned a spectacular golden-yellow as the sun slowly came up over the horizon. I finished my coffee all too soon and, thinking that I needed a bigger cup, headed back to camp, not really anxious to face the day's ordeals to come. Later, while trying to identify the location for new haul roads to be constructed, I came across a couple of old log cabins from the concentration camp era. I was amazed, since I was probably ten kilometers up the valley from the base camp. Further on up the hillside, I found an area with numerous old tree stumps, waist level in height. I concluded that the trees must have been cut during late winter when the snow depth would have been this high. Combined, the two sites were another reminder of the atrocities these prisoners had to endure. It was hard to imagine these poor souls being this far from the main camp, in subzero temperatures, having to cut down trees until they succumbed to the circumstances and died. One of my underlying fears at Siziman Bay was that we would construct a logging road and dig up some mass grave. Fortunately we never did.

I left camp at 6:45 p.m. on the evening of the twentieth with Chekinkov to catch the midnight train from Visakogorny to Komsomolsk. Due to various problems with the "Rooski Jeep" along the way, we missed the train by five minutes. As a result, it was off to Lydia's apartment to have some tea and wait for the next train at 2:15 a.m. Later when we returned to the station to get our tickets, there was no one around to purchase them from! When the train arrived, and we still had not been able to obtain tickets. Chekinkov and I rushed from one railcar to the next as he asked each attendant if any cabin was available. At the third railcar and with no luck on finding anything vacant, the attendant allowed us to jump on board as the train departed the station. As the train rattled its way down the tracks, we continued our quest until finally finding a couple of empty bunks, then paid the attendant for the tickets and settled in. When we arrived to Komsomolsk later that morning, a company driver was waiting for us in the parking lot to take me to the apartment. He returned in a couple of hours to take me to the office for a meeting with Phillipov and Chekinkov. That evening while sitting alone in the apartment, I raised a shot glass of vodka to what would have been my twentieth wedding anniversary—just for the hell of it.

The next day Misha, Andrei, and Sly came by the apartment at 6:30 p.m. to take me out on the town. "We'll have a party at one of my friend's place," Misha said, "but it doesn't start until 9:00." Since we had time to kill, we decided to start the evening off by having a couple of shots of cognac at a tiny bar called Marina near the sports stadium. When it was time to leave, Andrei flagged down a car to take us to the other side of town, stopping off first at a small store to purchase a few bottles of cognac, vodka, and wine. The party was at the apartment of Tatyana, or actually of her father who was out of town at the time. He apparently was involved in the oil business and as such, the furnishings indicated a higher-than-average affluence. Her brother Volody and another couple were also there.

We started the evening off with a huge meal consisting of various salads, vegetables, chicken, and, depending upon the individual's preference, cognac, vodka, beer, or wine. Misha began the first toast of the evening by introducing me to those who didn't already know me. At some point in the conversation, it came up that Tatyana was taking professional dance lessons. I commented that I loved to dance and considered myself fairly good at it. She laughed and, bragging about her expertise said, "I've been taking lessons for three years; I don't think you could keep up with me."

With this challenge, I turned to Misha and asked, "Is there somewhere we could go to continue this party and do some dancing?" He answered "sure!" and we quickly prepared to go. We took a relatively short walk to a favorite local bar of theirs called the Midnight Drugstore. Tatyana looked "hot," having changed into a short black skirt. Her black lace bra was visible through the tight mesh material of her form-fitting blouse. Black nylons and high heel shoes completed her outfit. She was definitely dressed to impress, and needless to say, I was impressed. Arriving at the bar, we ordered some drinks and stood listening to the music for a while. The place was packed, with a few couples out on the dance floor as the DJ played songs from his CD collection. I soon heard Misha's voice over the speaker system introducing me as "Paul, my good friend from the United States." Following this announcement, I didn't have to buy a drink for the rest of the night.

Tatyana eventually motioned to me that she wanted to dance, and taking my hand, led me out onto the floor. She slowly became impressed with my dancing ability, or perhaps it could have been all the alcohol she had been drinking. For whatever the reason, our bodies were soon so close together I don't think you could have slipped a dollar bill between us. Although very young, I have to admit that she felt pretty damn good. After a while, I left the bar with Misha to go outside and catch some fresh air while he had a smoke. Four young Russians followed us and immediately tried to pick a fight with me. We were just about to get into it when Andrei showed up which helped to even up the odds. After a few tense minutes, Misha and Andrei were able to calm them down and they left us alone, returning to the bar. I'm not sure what their problem was other than that they were drunk or perhaps that I was an American and they didn't like me dancing with Tatyana. Since it was 4:30 in the morning, we decided to return to the apartment. Once there, I crashed on one of the sofas and didn't wake up until after 10:30 a.m., an hour before Misha came back to life, sort of.

Misha was supposed to take his girlfriend, Lena, to the market that morning but didn't wake up until 11:30 a.m. He couldn't remember what time he was to meet her, so he didn't know if he was late or not. "Misha," I said, "you're probably late and most likely in trouble," so after having a quick cup of tea, we left to go find her. When we arrived at Lena's apartment, her mother informed us that she had already left for the local marketplace. With all the commotion going on, I was surprised that we were able to meet up with her. As we approached Lena, I had to admire Misha's taste in girlfriends. Lena was a tall, slender young woman with beautiful brown eyes, medium-length brown hair, and long shapely legs. Her continuous smile and pleasant personality made it easy to forget the lingering effects of the previous night. Misha, on the other hand, was hurting pretty bad from the previous night's drinking, and walking around in the hot sun wasn't helping him. It wasn't doing me any good either, since I left my hat back at Tatyana's place and as a result, the top of my head was fried.

Later in the day, as we walked along the river, Misha told me that he and Lena hoped to be able to purchase their own apartment in August. He commented that "we almost have enough money but need to borrow $500 from our friends." "Misha," I replied, "if you need it, I'd be happy to loan you the money." He took some offense when I said this, telling me that he "could get it from his Russian friends." "Don't give me that rich American having pity on a poor Russian bullshit," I said. "It is nothing more than an offer from one friend to another. Besides, I would expect you to pay me back." We left it at that and continued our walk until it was time for me to catch the train to Visakogorny.

Ron and Sharkoff were waiting for me at the train station, and after saying good-bye to Misha and Lena, I got on board. Once the train departed, Sharkoff pulled out a bottle of cognac, and of course, I couldn't refuse to have a couple of drinks with him. The three of us soon emptied the bottle, and I fell asleep, not waking again until just before arriving at Visakogorny at 2:30 a.m.

The *M/V Bulankan* was already in and being loaded when I got back into camp the morning of the twenty-fourth. Ivan, the captain, invited Joe and me down to the ship that evening for dinner, which consisted of salmon, salads, fried potatoes, etc.—and of course, beer and whiskey. Chuck and Genady came down after a while and joined us, as well as Ivan's girlfriend, Larissa, and Tatyana, a friend of hers from Vladivostok. The first mate, who turned out to be an excellent guitar player, entertained us with some classical Russian songs. I left the ship about nine-thirty with the party still going strong. Joe apparently got shit-faced drunk, as did Pritchard, and a couple of the ship's crew members had to help them off the vessel. Fortunately, they were able to climb into one of the log trucks that was being unloaded and hitch a ride back to the Gulag.

I felt guilty the next morning for sleeping in until eight o'clock. At least that was until I found out Joe was still in bed at 11:00 and Chuck didn't wake up until noon. I was having coffee in the Gulag lounge when Joe shuffled in. "You look like death warmed over," I commented as he poured some coffee. He just groaned in response and sat down at the table with me. "You old fart," I chuckled, "you going to survive?" "I'll never do that again," he replied, then chuckled as he lit up a cigarette. "You know," he said, "I can remember falling out of the log truck last night and at the time thinking, *Damn, I'm going to reinjure my shoulder.* But when I hit the ground, I was surprised. It felt soft and I didn't feel any pain!" Then, laughing as he spoke, "I realized that I'd landed on top of Pritchard who'd fallen out of the cab before me! You know," he continued after taking a sip of coffee, "I've said it before, but that Ivan really is the captain of a ship from hell!" We both laughed, and I answered, "You got that right." Just then, Chuck came in mumbling, "I need some coffee," and headed straight for the pot. After pouring a cup, he turned and in a raspy voice said, "Good morning, I think," then sat down with us.

The crew finished loading by early evening, and I watched the "ship from hell" steam southward as the *M/V Sibirskiy 2115* pulled into berth. Loading operations began by 9:00 p.m. Pritchard left camp to catch the early morning train to Komsomolsk to pack up the rest of his gear then head back to Seattle. Typical corporate procedure, the guy screwed up operations at Siziman Bay, was completely ineffective in the Komsomolsk office, and Frontier was sending him back to the States still under contract. He's gone, and now I was expected to salvage the operations and improve relationships with the Russians. Just amazing!

Joe was scheduled to fly out the next morning, so as the UAZ disappeared down the road I thought, *What better excuse than this to have a few drinks,* which is just what Joe and I did. After our third shot, Joe said, "Lord, I really need this trip out. I don't think I can spend another winter here; I'm getting too old for this." "Hey, I know," I replied, "but you'll feel better after some time out." "It's not just that, I'm tired of being alone," he continued. "What do you mean alone?" I joked. "You've got me here!" "Hell," he grumbled "I need someone I can cuddle up to, and it ain't going to be some damn Boy Scout!" Laughing, I offered one more drink for the road, and we both headed off to our rooms for the night.

I awoke the next day to news that one of the skidders and the D7 dozer were broke down. Subsequently, Chuck and Mike spent most of the day working out in the woods. Richard Nowlin made it into camp early this morning and spent most of the day resting up from his trip. The camp was covered by a thick fog all morning, giving way to thunderstorms during the afternoon. The helicopter that was scheduled to come in was unable to make the flight, so Joe had to take an evening crew bus into Visakogorny to catch the train for Khabarovsk. He was in exceptionally good spirits, looking forward to spending time in Homer, Alaska with his two daughters.

The water was absolutely flat the evening of the twenty-ninth, so I decided it was time to launch the C-Dory and do some fishing somewhere away from camp. Unexpectedly, the plug in the back of the transom had deteriorated so much that when the boat hit the water, it leaked like a sieve. By the time we got the boat back onto the trailer, there was over two inches of water on the floor. Fortunately, we found a spare plug which was in better condition than the first. After our minor delay and with an ample supply of beer on board, Chuck, Mike, Anatoly, and I headed north to explore the shoreline and search for more kumja. The coastline looked similar to areas of Alaska's Prince William Sound, fairly rugged and in its remoteness quite scenic. After about a half hour, we stopped at a small cove, started casting, and immediately caught fish. The area was full of kumja, and we continued to cruise the boat back and forth, casting toward shore as we went. I probably caught and released a dozen or more three-to-six-pounders.

A couple of days later, the guys and I said the hell with work and took the boat south to do some more fishing. During this trip, not only did we find lots of kumja, but on one of the gravel beaches, we found a number of Japanese glass floats. The beachcombing continued until John reached for a float and uncovered a hornets' nest in the driftwood. Screaming "bees," he took off running as if his life depended on it. Unfortunately, his unsuccessful attempt to outrun this angry swarm brought him right past me. I took off running in the opposite direction and fortunately was left unharmed. Back on the boat, John hooked into a fish which fought considerably harder than the kumja usually did. After perhaps fifteen minutes or more, he finally got it close enough to the boat for us to see that it was possibly a steelhead. Unfortunately, we did not have a net, and when I reached for the fish, it became unhooked and got away. Fortunately for me, Chuck grabbed on to my legs as I was slipping overboard and was able to pull me back onboard.

The last day of the month, as with crew change day on the first, was always slow for operations. I decided to take advantage of this and took Chuck out to inspect the new road being constructed over the mountain to access timber to the south. I had fought long and hard with the Russian engineers on where to locate this main haul road. My route was based on the map I made using the aerial photos I had obtained from the inventory foresters last year. Their initial route put the road through kilometer after kilometer of commercially worthless, dead beetle-killed timber and brush. I had attempted to take advantage of locating it through the few patches of live timber along the way to generate some exportable sawlog production to help offset costs.

Having won the argument, I now stood at the top of the pass, accepting Chuck's congratulations and reveling in my accomplishment. We popped the top off a couple of beers and enjoyed the view overlooking the Siziman River valley eastward toward the Strait, with the camp and jetty visible off in the distance. "You know Chuck" I commented while pointing to a group of dead spruce trees, "the Russians never will admit that it is beetles that are killing these trees. They call it *drying.*" "Drying?" he questioned. "Yah," I replied, "I've repeatedly told their foresters that I agree, and that of course the trees are drying. But it's the damn bugs that kill the trees and then they dry out! These are the same bugs killing thousands of acres of spruce forests in Alaska." Finishing our beers, I then said, "Chuck, why don't we top the day off by grabbing the other guys and taking the boat out for some more kumja?" "Sounds excellent," he replied, and we headed back to camp. By five o'clock, we were cruising south.

Although it was the Sunday back in the States, I telephoned George Bailey at his home early the next morning to inform him that I was considering not returning back to Siziman Bay after August. To my surprise, he sounded completely dumbfounded and asked me a lot of questions as to my reasoning for this. Most of my answers came back to actions that Cardinal did or did not do, such as not increasing my compensation when I became General Manager. "What? I authorized John to do this back in December," he exclaimed. I could sense his anger building as he continued "I thought this had been taken care of." George was very apologetic, finishing our conversation by saying, "I will be discussing this with John tomorrow morning and have him get back to you immediately."

The loading of the *Sibirskiy* was somewhat slower than usual, primarily due to equipment breakdowns, including the front-end log loader in the log yard. While I was down at the vessel watching operations, the captain informed me that he wanted to load at least 4,500 cubic meters. "Captain," I replied, "I can guarantee that we will load this vessel up to its full capacity. However," I continued, "since we are loading pulpwood, I doubt that we will exceed 4,100 cubic meters." Lena could not help but chuckle as the captain continued to argue with me on this issue. He was insistent, telling me, "You will load 4,500 cubic meters." I finally replied that "I will load logs until you direct me to stop," knowing that there was no way we'd obtain his goal. The captain smiled and, thinking that he had won the argument, turned and walked away. Lena broke out laughing as I looked at her and lifted my hands while shrugging my shoulders in a what-can-I-say gesture.

Later in the day, I decided to take a walk from the log sort yard over toward the Siziman River. While working my way through the waist-high grass, I came upon what was the site of a couple of the old Gulag buildings used for sleeping quarters. Each area had half a dozen small, iron bed frames placed side by side with no room in between. The bed frames were at best five feet long, so any normal person would be unable to stretch out their legs. The site was another stark, visual reminder of how miserable life—or more likely, slow death—was for these poor souls. That evening I was talking with Chekinkov about this. I told him that in the United States, we would be required to preserve Siziman Bay as a historical site. His solemn reply was that here they just wanted to bury the site and try to forget its past. And bury it they did, under tons of rock to form the base for the present-day camp and log yard.

The next morning when I answered the telephone, Cardinal abruptly asked, "What's up?" The tone in his voice, and that he didn't even bother to say hello, irritated me, so I began by updating him on the operations. When he finally brought up the subject of my conversation with Bailey and potential leaving, he offered me $120,000 per year retroactive to January first. "I'll fax over a new contract for you to sign and fax back," he continued. "I'll take a look at it and will consider my options," I replied. He called back an hour later and asked, "Have you read the contract?" "John," I answered, "we're right in the final stage of loading a ship. I won't have any time until later this evening." He angrily shouted back, "Well, make sure you read the fucking contract, and I'll call back tomorrow," then hung up. My immediate thought was, *And this asshole really thinks I want to continue working for him?*

Joe called from Khabarovsk shortly after my conversation with Cardinal. "How ya doing, buddy?" he asked, adding, "Do you miss me?" I answered, "you sound like you're in a good mood, what's up?" "Met a girl," he replied. "Already had two dinner dates and going out with her again tonight." "Ah hell, Joe," I jokingly responded, "you're just a horny, dirty old man." "You pot licker," he shouted. "I'm serious. From now on you can consider me a one-woman man."

Misha had come back into camp that morning and found me sitting at my desk reflecting on Joe's conversation. I mentioned it to him and that "Joe really got pissed off at me when I said he was just horny. I hope it's not too serious. I don't know, maybe he'll forget about her while he's back in the States." Misha commented, "Well you know Paul, every man needs a woman—even you." "Now don't you start with me on that," I chuckled. "By the way, it's good to see you. How are things back in Komsomolsk?" "Lena and I found an apartment to purchase," he replied. "All right," I exclaimed, "congratulations!" He hesitated, then asked, "Are you still willing to loan us $500?" "Absolutely," I answered, "no problem, be glad to do it." Obviously relieved, he said, "Thanks, Paul, it really means a lot to us." "Just remember," I said while slapping him on the back, "I do expect you to pay me back." Grabbing the bottle of vodka from the corner of my desk, I said, "Now let's have a couple of shots to seal the deal!"

Loading of the *Sibirskiy* was finally completed around noon with 4,164 cubic meters on board. Before I knew it, the vessel pulled away from the dock and anchored out in the bay. We still needed to have all the shipping documents signed, and I raised hell with the Russians for allowing the captain to depart. With Lena and Dmitry along, I attempted to take the C-Dory out to the ship, but about two-thirds of the way out was forced to turn back. Both Lena and Dmitry were scared to death. The swells were so big that even at a slow speed, the waves were breaking over the bow of the boat. I figured there would be no way we could tie up next to the vessel and climb up the rope ladder to board. On the way back in, some of the waves actually had the C-Dory surfing, and for a split second out of control. Once safely back onshore, I radioed the captain and informed him that I'd send someone to Vanino with the documents for signature upon his arrival to port.

I woke up at 4:00 a.m. the morning of the third in order to call the west coast and set up a translator for the trip with Chekinkov. There was a fax from Tokyo informing me of various issues regarding Osika Corporation. The bottom line was that we were loading the *M/V Dmitriev* with no agreed-upon customer, destination, or sales price. I sent a "nastygram" back to James telling him to inform Osika, and Takahara in particular that "if they do not accept this fucking cargo at our fucking price, they will not receive any more fucking shipments from Siziman Bay in the future." It was less than two hours before I was to leave camp, and I didn't need this frustration. To say the least, I was really pissed-off, but there was nothing I could do until getting to Khabarovsk.

The Russians farted around all morning and were late in getting the vehicle for me. I finally left camp at seven o'clock, and the driver turned what normally was a five-hour trip during this time of year into four hours. I ended up with some time to spare, so I spent about a half hour at Lydia Nikoliavich's apartment with her and Grisha. I had enough choot-choots of vodka with them to insure that I would fall asleep on the train, which I did with no problem, and I didn't wake up until 5:00 p.m. The weather was extremely warm and humid, making the railcar really hot inside. Many of the passengers stood out in the corridor with windows open, attempting to catch any possible refreshing breeze they could. Two cute little twin girls, maybe one and a half or two years old, ran up and down the length of the railcar. At one point both simultaneously tested their lung capacity for all to hear. Things didn't settle down until late at night, and I finally got back to a sound sleep around midnight.

The train arrived at Khabarovsk at 5:45 a.m., and I quickly caught a taxi—actually a private car—to the Parus Hotel. After checking in, I showered and shaved before going to the Shasta office where there was already a pile of faxes waiting for me. Osika Corporation got the message and had agreed to our sales prices, so everything was cleared for the *Dmitriev* shipment. Sergei, a Russian-American employee of Shasta, came into the office at 9:00 a.m. When I asked him, he confirmed that Joe had met a girl while here in Khabarovsk on his way back to the States, and that he "appeared to be in love.

She's about thirty-six years old, blonde hair, skinny, and doesn't speak any English." "For crying out loud, Sergei," I responded. "How in the hell can he fall in love if he can't even communicate with her?" Laughing, Sergei replied that "Joe mentioned they communicated quite well in bed, and that was all that mattered for now." "Doesn't surprise me," I said, "which just confirms what I've said: Joe is just an extremely lonely old man in need of some sex. I sure hope he will get this out of his system while back in Alaska with his two daughters." "I don't know about that," Sergei replied. "Joe told me he was thinking about coming back to Kabarovsk earlier than previously planned." I spent most of the day on the telephone to James in Seattle, Chuck at Siziman Bay, and Takahara in Tokyo, working out the shipment schedule for the remainder of July.

Chekinkov showed up at the hotel shortly after 7:00 a.m. the next morning. Our discussion was brief and without a translator. However, I understood that he would be going to the Dalny Resources office to freshen up. Although he and the driver were to be back at nine, by nine-thirty, thinking that I got our communications mixed up, I caught the hotel minivan to the airport. Andrei finally showed up just in time to purchase his ticket and get checked in for the flight. With our boarding passes in hand, we rushed to clear Customs and Immigration. As the officer checked my documents, I couldn't help but think *this was going to be a long week*. Amazingly enough, the plane departed Khabarovsk on time. It felt good to be going back to the States and, as I did every time, I asked myself; *Why in the hell do I keep going back?*

Six hours later, we touched down in Anchorage, Alaska where we were required to clear US Customs and Immigration. The immigration officer was the typical jerk with a poor, discriminatory attitude toward Russians. Not only did I have to explain what Andrei was doing in the United States, but I had to give the officer addresses for both our employers as well as the hotels we'd be staying at. I wrote the information down on a piece of paper and handed it to him. "Tonight I'll be staying at my parents' house," I explained, mildly irritated, "where I grew up at probably before you were even born. I don't believe you need their address." "Well," he responded, "we're tightening up on Russian visitors, although too late as far as I'm concerned. Too much Russian mafia coming and going." He finally cleared us for entry, and picking up our passports, I commented, "Your attitude sucks by the way, and it is not a good first impression of America."

The sun had always been on the horizon during the entire flight, and it was still fairly light outside when we exited the international terminal. We decided to walk the short distance to the domestic terminal rather than wait around for the shuttle bus. The flight to Seattle was on time, arriving at SeaTac airport at 5:30 a.m. I checked Andrei into the Hilton Hotel then went to Poulsbo to get my car, some cash, pay bills, say hello to my folks, and freshen up. I made it back to the Hilton in time to meet Elena and her daughter Sveta, our translator for the week. Andrei was still sleeping when I called, so Sveta and I made plans for the next day while we waited for him in the lobby. Once he came down, Elena drove us to her apartment for dinner.

Sveta came by the hotel early the next morning and, like a true Russian, insisted she take us back to the apartment and cook us breakfast. After finishing, we said good-bye to Elena, and the three of us left to catch the ferry from Seattle across Puget Sound to Bainbridge Island. Since it was Saturday, I had decided to take Chekinkov up to Hurricane Ridge in the Olympic National Park. On the way there, I drove through Poulsbo to show him where I grew up as a kid. We briefly stopped by my parents' place to introduce Andrei to them, and in part, to jokingly let my dad see who he had worked to protect us from for all those years after the war. Leaving Poulsbo, we drove north through the historic logging-sawmill town of Port Gamble then over the Hood Canal Bridge and on to Port Angeles. It was early afternoon by the time we made it up into the Park.

I quickly found a vacant table in the picnic area. Sveta and her mother had prepared a huge picnic lunch with barbeque chicken and all the other standard Russian fixings. Andrei enjoyed feeding the pesky jays and became excited when a beautiful three-point deer slowly walked out of a clump of trees. He was in awe as the deer cautiously approached him and nibbled at a carrot being offered. Chekinkov had a huge smile on his face as the deer casually walked away. He commented that, "This is so amazing that you can get so close to the animals here." He chuckled, adding that "anything that is edible in the Russian wild gets shot." After leaving Hurricane Ridge, we drove down the west side of Hood Canal where Chekinkov, stripping down to his black briefs, and Sveta, in her shorts and bra, went swimming at a State Park south of Hoodsport.

The next day, Chekinkov was too tired to do anything but sleep, which is what he ended up doing. After having breakfast at the hotel, since I didn't have anything else to do, I took Sveta to the Pt. Defiance Zoo in Tacoma. She had lived three years in the Seattle area and had never been there. Later that afternoon we took Andrei to the Southcenter Mall so he could do some shopping. I couldn't help but laugh to myself as he checked out the women's lingerie in Victoria's Secret for one of the accountants back in Komsomolsk. Sveta was embarrassed but patient, as Andrei would occasionally hold a bra and matching panties up against her to check out how they looked. "Andrei," I joked, "when I see Marina at the office, I'm going to ask her which color she is wearing." He placed his finger to his lips, then made me promise to keep quiet about all this.

On Monday I took Chekinkov to a timber harvest operation near Chehalis and observed the type of equipment I was recommending for Siziman Bay operations. Tuesday it was out to a site located toward Mt. Rainier. On Wednesday, we caught a 7:00 a.m. flight to Spokane to meet up with Hubert and look at an operation in that area. Hubert had also coordinated a tour of the Potlatch plywood facility for us. Before going back to the hotel, we stopped at Hubert's property on the St. Joe River where Chekinkov and Sveta cooled off in the river. I didn't feel like swimming, so Hubert and I sat on the riverbank and talked while having some beers.

Early the next morning, it was off to Portland, Oregon, on a Horizon Airlines flight to meet up with Newton. Our designated meeting place was some small truck scaling area on the Sunset Highway; however, I somehow missed it, and we ended up at Seaside. Neither of them had ever seen the Pacific Ocean before. Since it was too late to see the logging process, I decided what the hell, we'd stay at the beach, and I told them to enjoy the beach and go swimming. Chekinkov commented that "this is like going to a resort." He was afraid though that he would get in trouble with his superiors back in Russia, so "please do not tell anyone about this." He also didn't want me to mention anything about going to Hurricane Ridge, even though it was on the weekend and I didn't have any business trip lined up. It seemed like the entire working class people in Russia lived in constant fear of retribution and/or punishment. Back in the Seattle area the next day, Sveta went with Chekinkov for more shopping while I took Joe Dill to the doctor then over to Poulsbo to put my car back into storage. Once we returned to SeaTac, Joe quickly left for Portland to visit with his daughters. Sveta and I went with Andrei to assist in getting him checked-in and on his flight back to Russia. Poor Sveta ended up having to assist the ticketing agent in translating for a dozen or so other Russians attempting to check-in as well. With Chekinkov finally onboard his plane, I said goodbye to Sveta then headed to the nearest bar for a quick drink to relax before walking back to the hotel for the night.

I caught a flight to Japan the next day and the plane touched down at the Tokyo-Narita Airport around 4:30 p.m. on the fourteenth. No one was there to meet me, so after wandering around in a mass of Japanese travelers, I was finally able to figure out which train would get me to the Akasaka Station nearest my hotel. Sergei Phillipov, Dmitry Sharkoff, Jeff, and Takahara were already there and heard me getting into my room. They all came out into the hallway to greet me, and after placing my bags inside, it was off to Sergei's room for some vodka choot-choots. This was really the last thing I needed to do after a long flight, but as usual I couldn't refuse.

At around 10:00 p.m., I finally convinced them that I needed to go have some dinner, and I went downstairs to the restaurant with Jeff. Soon Takahara and Oseki, another Osika Corporation employee, came down and joined us. The next thing I knew, Takahara ordered a round of double shots of cognac. In the morning, Takahara told me he couldn't remember very much about the previous night, which didn't surprise me. Since he couldn't recall coming down to the restaurant, I jokingly told him that he owed me big time for the cognac he ordered which cost me twenty dollars a glass. He then informed me that Oseki, who was driving the boss's car at the time, got arrested by the police and taken to the station. He was looking at a possible $400 fine and the loss of his driver's license for a month! All I could say was, "Ouch!"

After four days of traveling around Japan, meeting with customers, and looking at various port operations, we left Tokyo on an early-morning shinkansen to Niigata. Although they had been shopping every day, Sergei and Dmitry wanted to have enough time to do some additional shopping in Niigata before catching the 3:30 p.m. Aeroflot flight back to Khabarovsk on the nineteenth.

While filling out his customs declaration form for re-entry into Russia, Sergei had apparently miscounted his US dollars and identified the amount incorrectly. When the Customs Agent in Khabarovsk checked this, she came up one hundred dollars short and immediately began to hassle him about it. Sergei turned to me and asked if I had any dollars. I hadn't really paid too much attention to what was going on, but I should have, because when I showed him my cash, Sergei quickly grabbed a one-hundred-dollar bill and slipped it into his pocket. Then, pulling it back out of his pocket he showed it to the Agent and cleared Customs. Since my one-hundred-dollar-bill left the Customs area with Sergei, I was now one hundred dollars short on my declaration. However the Agent, having seen that Sergei had taken my bill, and knowing that I was an American, smiled then politely asked me to change the amount on my declaration. After clearing Customs, I walked out into the airport lobby, and Sergei handed my one hundred dollars back to me.

The next day, after having a long telephone conversation with Cardinal about continuing on at Siziman Bay, I telephoned Basil and accepted his offer as Manager, Russian Operations. I then faxed my letter of termination to the Philadelphia office and headed down to the park area along the Amur River. I just couldn't see myself working with such an idiot as Cardinal anymore and needed to get out of the office to reflect on my future. As I stood on the walkway, drinking my beer and watching the people enjoying the extremely hot, muggy day, I noticed two attractive young bikini-clad women standing in the river locked in an embrace and kissing. Surprised to see such passionate affection between lesbians openly exhibited in public in Russia, I felt like vomiting. I could only think, *What a waste of such beautiful women.* Later that evening, I was on the 10:00 p.m. train to Komsomolsk for what I thought would be my last trip out to Siziman Bay. Fortunately, the air conditioning was for once working, and I was able to get a decent night's sleep.

Upon arriving into Komsomolsk at seven o'clock the next morning, I was immediately taken to the office. The place was in turmoil with the employees scurrying about in a panic mode. Apparently Nazarkin was in Philadelphia on another rampage and was threatening to fire Phillipov, Sharkoff, Chekinkov, and Potarov. From what I could gather, someone had sent a fax to the States and the message got incorrectly translated to imply that nobody at Siziman Bay and/or Komsomolsk knew what they were doing.

Misha came by the apartment later in the afternoon, and I gave him the $500 that he and Lena needed to purchase the apartment they wanted. We then went down to the river to have a couple of beers and BS. During the past year, although considerably younger than I, we had developed a deep friendship for each other. We also discussed having Sveta come to meet me to talk about working for Shasta in Vladivostok. I knew that Dalny-Les treated her poorly but was surprised to learn that she was only paid an equivalent to $150 per month. It was no wonder she felt it necessary to shack up with one of the asshole Russians in Visakogorny just to survive. She was excited about the opportunity to break away from this no-win situation, and I was happy to be able to help her out. She was a hard and conscientious worker and deserved a real chance to get ahead.

That asshole Cardinal got to Sergei about my resignation before I could. He and everyone else was really upset about my decision and tried to convince me to change my mind and stay on. I tried to keep my reasoning from being too personal, but they all knew that the primary issue was with Cardinal himself. "I will telephone Cardinal tomorrow morning and discuss the situation with him directly," Sergei said before leaving the office. I couldn't help thinking that as difficult as it was to turn down an offer of $120,000 per year, retroactive to the first of January, I just couldn't see working with Cardinal any longer. The man was just not straight forward with anyone, including the Russians, the expats at Siziman Bay, Shasta Corporation, and even his superiors at Frontier. I went through hell with a manager like that in Alaska, and I did not feel that I could survive physically or mentally going through that type of situation again. My health had declined significantly during the previous three months, and something had to change. The one thing I did know was that I was looking forward to going back to the States in a couple of weeks and spending time with the kids.

A few days later as I walked up the small tributary stream to the Siziman River, I wished that I had brought my fly rod. At every pool, trout would dart for cover as I approached. In all my years of working in the forest products industry, I had never been too concerned about my being out in the forest by myself. Even in my years working in remote areas of Alaska, I spent countless hours working alone without much thought. However, as I looked at the bear track left in the sand, an uneasy feeling came over me. This footprint was comparable in size to any of those I had seen in Alaska. The difference was that, here in Russia, I was not able to carry my standard .375 H & H Magnum rifle and/or Smith & Wesson 44 Magnum pistol. I don't know, why but up until this point, I never really thought about bears being in this region. This track changed my way of thinking, and as a result, I started making a little more noise as I continued up the valley. This would be my last trip out into the forest at Siziman Bay, and back at the truck, I couldn't help but feel a slight sense of sadness about this.

Later that evening, I grabbed a bottle of cognac and walked down to the beach. I was tired of people trying to convince me to stay and just wanted to be alone with my thoughts. The evening air had a chill, but a couple of shots of cognac helped to keep me warm. I sat silently listening to the waves gently lapping at the shoreline. A seal suddenly broke the peace as it surfaced violently, thrashing about with a salmon held tightly in its mouth. With the fish losing its battle for life, the seal again submerged to continue its search for another meal, and calm once again came over the area. The evening light faded as the darkness of night drew nearer. Pouring some more cognac into my glass, I had the sense that I truly was going to miss this place. With my shot glass raised toward the jetty, I silently gave a toast to Siziman Bay and the many friends that I had made over the past year. I then had one more shot before walking back to camp. Two days later, I was on the Alaska Airlines flight back to the States.

One month later, I was back in Khabarovsk sitting at my desk in the comfortable air-conditioned office that Shasta Corporation had in the Parus Hotel. I felt enthusiastic about the new direction my life was taking and the business opportunity I had been given. As I sipped on my freshly brewed Seattle's Best coffee, I watched Olga in her short miniskirt move about the room. I smiled as I wondered if I'd really be able to concentrate on anything other than her fine figured body and beautiful, long legs. Finally, I thought, my life had returned to some sense of normality. If only I had known how wrong I was and what experiences the future was going to bring. . . . But that's another story.

About the Author

Paul Tweiten earned a bachelor's degree in forest management from the University of Washington. Involved in the forest products industry in Russia for over fifteen years, Tweiten has traveled throughout the Russian Far East and Siberia. He is president of Pacific Forest Products Inc., a company he started in 2003. He currently lives in Washington.